**CHUC**
**MERRY**

Photo credit: Christopher Francis

Khyrunnisa A. is an award-winning author of children's fiction. Her first book for adults—the bestselling collection of essays, *Tongue In Cheek: The Funny Side of Life*—continues to regale readers. She is a full time author and lives in Thiruvananthapuram.

Visit her at: www.khyrunnisa.com
Write to her at: khyrubutter@gmail.com

## Praise for *Tongue in Cheek*

'*Tongue in Cheek* offers a humorous take on everyday occurrences that often pass by unnoticed.... Anecdotal and relatable, Khyrunnisa's stories shine with wit.' – *The Telegraph*

'In Ms Khyrunnisa's present collection, that shows up a funny mirror to the whole range of the "ordinary life-world," there is a faint Stephen Leacock touch of direct, sharp, yet enjoyable and tasteful humour in the days of cultural trolling in social media.' – *The Deccan Chronicle*

'These easy-to-relate-to short stories are written around incidents that we encounter on a daily basis but taking them to a whole new level.' – *The Asian Age*

'Peppered with relatable instances and keeping the drama to a believable limit, Khyrunnisa has crafted an entertaining piece with some side-splitting stories.' – *The New Indian Express*

'*Tongue in Cheek* records the semi-autobiographical travails of an urban woman and her witty observations on day-to-day life.' – *The Hindu*

'*Tongue in Cheek* is the perfect companion after a stressful day.' – *Outlook*

# CHUCKLE MERRY SPIN

## Us in the U.S.

# Khyrunnisa A.

First published by Westland Books, a division of Nasadiya Technologies Private Limited, in 2022

No. 269/2B, First Floor, 'Irai Arul', Vimalraj Street, Nethaji Nagar, Allappakkam Main Road, Maduravoyal, Chennai 600095

Westland and the Westland logo are the trademarks of Nasadiya Technologies Private Limited, or its affiliates.

ISBN: 9789395073028

10 9 8 7 6 5 4 3 2 1

Typeset by SÜRYA, New Delhi

Printed at Nutech Print Services - India

*For*
*Amar and Arpitha—A & A*
*Who kept us out of trouble in the U.S.A.*

# Contents

# Author's Note

WHO SAID THE U.S. is not an exotic holiday destination any longer? That the days when a trip to the U.S. was replete with adventure, uncertainty, thrills and chills are long gone? Believe me, it becomes all that and more when two Luddites land in that country on their debut trip abroad.

Yes, debut trip. I'm not kidding. Until my husband and I went to the U.S. in 2018, we hadn't ventured outside India, not even to nearby countries. Armchair travel and listening goggle-eyed to pulsating stories of other people's expeditions to foreign lands had been our favoured and safe mode of tourism. We were happy to let our neighbouring countries be. No crossing the seas to stomp through Sri Lankan forests or to laze on the beaches of Maldives for us. No desire to go clambering all over the mountains of Bhutan or Nepal. And we magnanimously left the UAE to thousands of others.

Then, the impossible happened. 'You MUST come to Syracuse for my graduation.' Thus spake Arpitha, the daughter-in-law. Over the phone, of course, but that was enough; it worked like magic. The wheels of overseas travel began to spin like crazy and soon we were in the U.S. This was in 2018, though, before the Covid 19 virus threw a spanner into all impromptu travel plans.

The U.S. is beautiful. We discovered that first-hand during our forty-day sojourn in the country. But it did take some getting used to. We had to remember a few simple basics. That we were actually breathing fresh air. That a queue meant standing a few paces behind the person in front, not adjacent to them. That walking was always on the right, even in the mega corridors of shopping malls. That the groaning and creaking houses we visited were not haunted but made of wood. That walls had ears. That multiple switches were scarce. That switches in homes and hotels were upside down and rarely near beds or doors. That passages were often dark, and locating the upside down switches was an adventure in itself. That restrooms had paper, not water. And that 'Big' was the operative word—everything, like the country itself, was giant-sized.

However, it was the heavy reliance on technology that stumped us. If you think a visit to a First World country is a walk in the park because of the many facilities it has, you have another think coming. You can't afford to be technologically challenged if you want to use those facilities. We were. But so what? We had a tech-savvy son and daughter-in-law to take care of all that and help us out of scrapes—technology-related or otherwise. We had warm friends to host us and take us around. And thus we blundered our way through many parts of the U.S.—landing in Chicago, going to Syracuse, cruising from Boston in the East Coast to California in the west, before wending back, and many other places in between. We had a wonderful time through it all.

This light-hearted travelogue recounts the eventful and enjoyable forty days we spent in the U.S. I'm not sure if St Augustine got it right when he said, 'The world is a book, and those who do not travel read only a page.' But I hope you read all the pages of this book and indifferent travellers are encouraged to travel and go places, literally. With all safety precautions and shots in place, of course. And be sure to have a smart phone with you. Or a smart son and daughter-in-law.

Khyrunnisa A.
2022

# The Travel Bug Bites

'GO ABROAD? NO WAY!' protested my husband, Vijaya Kumar, who will henceforth be called VK. 'Why, we don't even have passports, and I have asthma.' These were the stock excuses he offered for his decision to stick to Thiruvananthapuram like chewing gum on footwear.

The very idea of travelling abroad, or travelling anywhere, in fact, is anathema to him.

And if misguided friends or relatives persisted in trying to make him change his mind, he would come up with the clincher, 'Going out of Thiruvananthapuram is like going abroad.'

That is exactly how he feels too. VK's attachment to the city is legion. He is, among other things, a great armchair traveller who is probably better informed about most countries than their natives; who believes that the best way to see exciting new countries is through the eyes of books. As for me, the prospect of travel doesn't exactly fire me up. I like visiting new places, but I hate the idea of packing and travelling. How wonderful if I could reach a destination at the press of a button. Since that is too much to expect even in a technologically hyper-advanced world, I'm fine with digging my feet in and staying put.

After facing such unexpected opposition, people would generally leave us alone—tight-fisted scrooges, they must have concluded in private. Old stick-in-the-muds, or, is it sticks-in-the-mud? But a daughter-in-law is a different ball game, much harder to deter than other beings. Arpitha, our daughter-in-law, who was pursuing her MS in Syracuse University, called one day to say that she and Amar, my son, wanted us to attend her graduation. 'Please, Aunty, you must come!' She calls us 'Aunty' and 'Uncle', by the way, for that was how she used to address us before her marriage and felt more comfortable continuing with those familiar appellations. We were pleased, and secretly relieved; we found the new roles of in-laws a little daunting.

'I'd be delighted,' I responded, my face breaking into a broad grin. Wasted, for she couldn't see me. 'But there's someone else to be reckoned with. The one who can tilt the scales.' Then, I have to confess, we plotted a bit. 'Ask Uncle. And keep asking,' I advised.

But, as it turned out, such persistence wasn't necessary. The next evening, she called him, and, without any lead up, announced, 'Uncle, my graduation ceremony is on May 12.'

I was hovering about, eavesdropping shamelessly. 'Amazing!' VK responded, all smiles. He was oblivious to our wiles. 'Brilliant!' he continued, with boyish enthusiasm. He would have clapped his hands if his left hadn't been holding the phone. He added a couple more adjectives, and was preparing to unleash the rest, probably in alphabetical order, but Arpitha must have interrupted him, for he stopped talking and started listening.

Next, I heard him say, 'Let me see.' Did I hear that

right? I shook my head in disbelief. Amar, our son, had long been urging us to visit him while he was working on site in the U.S. He invited us when he was in Boston, and he's been inviting us after moving to Wisconsin. But all those invitations fell on deaf ears—VK 's, not mine.

And now, after five years, VK was actually considering going. Oh, the irresistible charms of a daughter-in-law! He hadn't even demurred, and we capitalised on that. Arpitha is a smart, sensible girl with a no-nonsense approach to life. Persistence is her middle name. She had been prepared for a long battle and was delighted when she elicited this response from him. Amar was thrilled too. Now that the resistance had been dismantled, it was just a question of finalising the details.

This paved the way for the next part of the plan. VK began to be bombarded with calls from the U.S. Amar and Arpitha (A&A) took turns to call daily. 'Have you applied for a passport yet?' 'What's happening?' 'No time to waste.' 'The visa process takes a long while.' 'Don't forget, my graduation is on May 12.' 'Please hurry.'

Poor VK's non-committal, 'Let me see', had been interpreted as 'Yes', and there was no going back.

The wheels to travel to the U.S. were set into motion. The first hurdle to be crossed was that of getting our passports. To our delighted surprise, it turned out to be no hurdle at all. And to think we had been using that as an excuse for not venturing abroad when the whole process was ridiculously easy and hassle-free. But how on earth were we to know? No one had ever disputed our excuse, but that could have been because they had all got their passports a long time back, when securing one had been fraught with adventure, suspense, chewed fingernails and inordinate delays caused by morale-sapping encounters with the bureaucracy.

Our experience was painless. VK has always been a thorough investigator and I wasn't surprised to find him huddled over the computer, doing an intensive search on the internet—where else?—for information on getting a passport. If only we could do a Google search for misplaced keys, glasses, bank passbooks and phones on silent mode.

After an hour of peering into the screen and opening a row of new tabs, he looked up and declared, 'We must go to the passport office.' I was about to say, 'Really? I thought we'd need to go to the ration shop', when he added, 'but it's wiser to consult an authorised travel agent first.' Hmm, that made sense.

In three days flat, the passports arrived by speed post— we went, we applied and we succeeded.

A quick word on the efficiency of the passport office. The Passport Seva Kendra is maintained by the Tata Consultancy Services, under the eagle eyes of an official appointed by the central government. TCS was given this responsibility in 2008, as part of the Government of India policy to facilitate and speed up the passport issuance system. It has worked wonders.

But don't be fooled into thinking this is a welcome glimpse of new India. All you need to do is visit a 'village office', the city corporation office, or any number of other government agencies meant to 'serve' the public, to understand that the old India is not only doing well, but is flourishing.

The travel agency also had a significant role to play in helping us get our passports. This encouraged us to go to another established travel agency for the visa process. These agencies are a boon to clueless people like us, and once we had provided all the documents required—an invitation letter from Arpitha for the graduation, another one from Amar ('Dear parents, I'd be deeply obliged if you grace my apartment in the U.S. with a visit ...'), his rent receipts, bank statements and so on—in no time, we were choosing dates for the consulate visit in Chennai.

We had to pick the time too, for the interview days were divided into several 15-minute slots. After some deliberation, we decided on 1 p.m. on 14 March for our biometrics and 9 a.m. on 15 March for the interview at the consulate. The travel agent got us our appointment letters for the confirmed dates and also gave us a file each with all the documents placed in neat order. Most importantly, he gave us invaluable briefing on how to talk or how not to talk at the interview. 'Don't answer any questions they don't ask.' 'Don't volunteer any information not required.' In other words, don't be chatty—fitting advice for college teachers.

In three weeks, we were in Chennai for our interview, staying at the apartment of VK's cousin, Prithvi. On the day scheduled for our biometrics, Prithvi dropped us off at 12.25 p.m. for a 1 p.m. appointment; we had never been this early for any appointment before this. Since nothing except our persons and our files were allowed in, we gave Prithvi our phones, bags and all our earthly belongings. 'I'll wait somewhere ahead,' he pointed vaguely at the sky, and drove away.

Imagine our surprise when not only were we allowed in early—a welcome breach—everything was over by 12.45. We couldn't believe our luck and jauntily bounded out, only to realise we had rejoiced too soon. Prithvi and his car were nowhere in sight. We went up and down the street, and looked into side lanes and alleys too. I even looked up at the sky, remembering his sign off before he drove away. That we didn't know the number of the car made the search futile. Finally, good sense prevailed, and we decided to wait where he had dropped us.

Sweat was pouring down our faces as we took position at our designated spot. A woman selling tender coconuts, detecting thirsty throats and potential business, asked if we wanted coconuts. We wanted a phone, we said. Her husband immediately delved into his underwear, under his lungi, and brought out a small phone. But alas, Prithvi's number was saved in our phones' memory, not ours, and both phones were in his possession. We made calls to the only numbers we knew by heart—our own—but the honourable Prithviraj who didn't believe in intruding on people's privacy, refused to take them. We gave up and since the other honourable man, the coconut seller's husband, wouldn't accept money for the calls that hadn't gone through, we did the next best thing—bought tender coconuts from his wife. At 1.15, Prithvi appeared, a happy smile plastered on his face. 'Ha! Out so soon? Miracle! I'd gone to meet friends,' he said breezily. We gave him weak smiles and crawled into the car.

The next morning found me quite on edge; it was the day of the all-important interview. I hadn't felt so apprehensive even for my job interview. Keeping to our new-found enthusiasm for reaching destinations ahead of time, we arrived at the consulate at a healthy 8.30 a.m. only to find a long, undulating queue already formed and growing longer by the second. We hurried to the end, but unsure if we should join or enquire about the situation, our appointment being slated for 9 a.m., dithered. That hesitation cost us our place in the line. Four others joined while we scratched our heads.

We discovered, to our consternation, that others ahead of us had appointments for 9.15 and 9.30. Now what? VK, patient as ever, said we should wait. But I was worried. What if we missed the appointment? We were so far away from the entrance, how would we even hear our slots being announced? At 8.45 I told VK that I'd go to the gate to enquire, while he held my place. I approached the entrance just in time to hear a man announce, 'All 9 a.m. interviewees come to the right, 8.45 to the left and the others, please wait.'

I managed to catch VK's eye and waved to him to come forward. A few others gleefully came along too. We were relieved to be in the right queue. Looking around, I was surprised to see a guy who had earlier told me his appointment was at 9.30, waiting in the 8.45 queue. When those in that line were called in, he jumped to our queue. When it was our turn, the jumping jack leaped to the 9.15 line. I bet this human grasshopper would have managed to be the first in his legitimate 9.45 queue. Not that it would have given him any specific advantage, but he belongs to the breed that has an inbuilt compulsion to cut queues for that single minute's advantage.

Once in, we were sent from one section to another. Everything was moving with amazing efficiency. We were searched, our IDs were checked, fingerprinting was done again and finally we were given the number of a counter for our interview. Hearts in our mouths, we hurried there to find an interview going on. Of course we listened, ears flapping, hoping to get a few on the spot tips on what to say and what to withhold. We found out what not to say all right.

The elderly man who was being interviewed was the picture of uncertainty, hemming and hawing, while his wife stood silently by. We gathered that he had three sons in the U.S. but couldn't tell the woman interviewing him in which part of the country they lived. Asked why he was visiting the U.S., he mumbled, 'Religious reasons.' Uh oh! The last thing he should have said. The interviewer pricked up her ears. 'Religious?' And he responded, 'Yes, we're going for our grandchild's baptism.' She asked him again where his sons lived, but he didn't seem to know the states, leave alone the addresses. Poor man, his three sons should have tutored him better or he should have taken a short correspondence course from our travel agent. VK and I could chant Amar's residential address backwards in our sleep.

The woman wished him well and returned his passport. Our hearts sank when we saw that. We knew that a passport returned is a visa denied. In fact, I had been surreptitiously glancing at the people walking away after their interviews at various counters. Their faces and files told their story—happy faces had no passports in their files while sad-faced ones were obviously weighed down by their disappointment and their passports.

Bewildered, the man offered it back. She said they'd inform him if he needed to hand it in. Now he realised something wasn't right. He took out the passport-sized photographs of him and his wife from his shirt pocket as if to say, 'If you don't want the passports, then take the passport-sized photos. Take something, anything!' The woman politely but firmly refused to accept them and he turned away, looking rather upset. It was clear his visa application had been rejected.

Meanwhile, I was also watching the diverting scene at the next counter where a woman was being interviewed. She didn't know English, only Tamil, so an American interpreter had been provided to assist her. It was clear she couldn't make any sense of his heavily Americanised Tamil while he couldn't understand her dialectal Tamil and they were talking at cross purposes:

He: 'Why are you going to the U.S.?'

She: 'I'm very happy to meet you, sir.'

He: 'How long do you want to stay in the U.S.?'

She: 'I've been married for five years and my husband drinks.'

When we were called, I followed VK to the counter with a deep sense of regret that I couldn't be a witness all the way. Stand-up comedians could have picked up a few hints. My guess is that the woman must have been given the visa, while VK believes she'd have been denied it. It remains a matter of speculation.

We reached the counter, a little nervous, having just witnessed a visa application being turned down. Now we could see the interviewer clearly. She was a friendly

American of Asian descent, probably Korean. I knew if she decided to reject our application, she'd convey the news with a cheerful smile, as if she were conferring an award on us.

I stood behind my husband, like a good Indian wife, but a little to the side so that I was visible, and let him do all the talking. She asked him what subject he taught and repeated the question to me. I repeated the answer for we had both taught English. Very good Indian wife, she must have thought.

Now came the big question. 'Why are you going to the U.S.?' When VK said it was for our daughter-in-law's graduation, she nodded in appreciation. 'That's excellent. So won't she be looking for a job now that she is graduating?'

Had I been answering the question, I might have played right into her hands. The U.S. is wary of students from abroad sticking on there after graduation. 'Of course!' I'd have gushed. 'Why, she's already got a couple of interviews lined up.'

But my smart husband, who can think on his feet, replied without batting an eyelid, 'Maybe, but right now she's very excited about her graduation,' sounding pretty fired-up himself. Now I understood. What a neat side-tracking of that pertinent question.

The excitement was catching, and the woman smiled broadly. 'So, who's paying for your tickets?' VK drew himself up to his full height—all of 5 feet and a few inches—and declared, 'My son wanted to finance the trip, but we said we'd buy our tickets.' At this, she laughed outright. 'Great. Then why don't you buy mine too?' What? Was she actually joking? I felt a huge sense of relief that the interview was going in the right direction. Good cheer and bonhomie all around. VK smiled. 'I wouldn't mind doing that at all.'

Now she beamed. 'Congratulations, your visa has been approved. Have a safe journey and best wishes to your daughter-in-law.'

By 9.50 we were out. When Prithvi had dropped us at the consulate, he said he'd wait at the graveyard in the church close by. The U.S. consulate is actually built on land leased from the cathedral. A grim choice, but you couldn't have asked for a more specific rendezvous. So much better than that vague, 'I'll be there somewhere' of the previous day. Who can miss a graveyard, or be missed at one unless you are a ghost? I expected to find Prithvi perched on one of the graves when we reached there, leaning comfortably on a headstone, checking his phone.

There was no Prithvi in sight. Instead, we were met by a host of British graves—some with ornate tombstones, others with simpler ones that only gave the names and broad details of the deceased. It was a solemn, cool and beautiful place. We walked about the graveyard that was a part of St George's Cathedral and learnt it was one of the earliest Anglican churches in India, built in 1815. We added to our general knowledge, but after we went around it twice, peering at tombs and exclaiming over the artistry of the stonework that stood as testimony to long dead people, the morbidity of the surroundings got to me. What on earth were we doing pottering about these graves, impressive though they were?

The atmosphere was ideal to inspire a script for a

spooky movie or a melancholic poem on mortality, death and decay—the poet Thomas Gray would have revelled in it. But really! We had just got good news and wanted to celebrate. How do you dance a joyful jig among tombs? And where was Prithvi? At this point we noticed a couple in the distance. The man looked at me and what he held in his hand set my pulse racing. No, it wasn't a red rose, but a mobile phone. We struck up a conversation with them, and he willingly loaned us his phone. This time we had grown wiser, and VK had Prithvi's phone number and a few others written on a slip of paper, in his pocket. We called Prithvi who came soon after, saying he had been waiting for our call. Oh, Prithvi!

We returned to Thiruvananthapuram and very soon, received our passports stamped with the visa valid for ten years. U.S.A., here we come!

# Raring to Go

DID THE U.S. HAVE TO be so far away from India? Imagine, having to fly nineteen hours to reach Chicago. Yikes! All because Christopher Columbus couldn't sit at home and follow his father's wool trade like a good boy. Ah, well, no point wool gathering about re-inventing history to suit your convenience. Now that we had our visas, we had to think of booking tickets. There's no direct flight from Thiruvananthapuram to Chicago—you have to change flights at least once. We toyed with the option of going via Frankfurt since it would divide the journey into two flights of more or less equal duration, only to drop it in double-quick haste when we found it would be twice as expensive as going via Dubai.

Emirates became the popular choice and we booked tickets to go to Dubai and thereon to Chicago. Though it meant one short flight of four and quarter hours followed by the much dreaded mega-long fifteen-hour flight to O'Hare International Airport, we felt ridiculously pleased we had saved a lot of money.

We picked our seats too, paying extra for a two-seater row rather close to the back in both aircrafts, for we didn't want people crawling all over us to stretch their legs or go to the toilet. We also hoped it would give us some privacy during the long flight and our cavernous snoring mouths wouldn't tempt a brat seated close by to drop in a rolled paper napkin, chewed gum or something worse. On the advice of the admirable travel agent, we also took health insurance to cover the duration of our trip for health care costs a bomb in the U.S. And since we didn't have an occasion to test it out, I can say it worked like a charm. The flight formalities done, we turned our attention to packing.

Anyone who called would ask if we had finished packing—what on earth. Do people actually pack a month in advance? Apparently, they do; procrastinators like us are the exceptions. So, when we did start, we went into it with the enthusiasm of children getting ready for the new academic year in school—new clothes, new bags, new shoes, new umbrellas ... Unsure of what clothes to pack, I appealed to Arpitha for help, and after some thought, she suggested six salwar suits for the forty-day visit. She hesitated before adding, 'Maybe a pair of jeans too.' She was probably unsure how the mother-in-law whom she called 'Aunty' would take that recommendation. The mother-in-law jumped at it—she had been waiting for a reason to jump into jeans. I promptly bought two pairs. I packed a saree too, for Arpitha's graduation; I thought the special occasion warranted a formal Indian attire.

With great reluctance, VK also got himself one. A pair of jeans I mean, not a saree. He isn't a great fan of jeans and was determined to take only trousers to the U.S. but, sensing this, Amar called to reel off the recommending features of jeans—'They keep you warm in the cold weather, they're good for rough use and one pair of jeans goes a long way.' That clinched it. We were going a long way anyway. But VK couldn't find the perfect pair. Slim, skinny jeans that looked like jodhpurs or low-rise jeans that were sure to tempt fate and invite sniggers were the rage. He turned them all down.

'Distressed, sir?' the salesperson asked, displaying a pair of jeans that looked like a tramp's discard.

'Very,' VK replied, looking unhappy. The puzzled guy backed off and we left the store to go on a 'decent jeans' hunt. Finally, we found a pair that met with his hesitant approval—it was okay, mostly, but he was unhappy about the elastic at the sides. 'To fit well, sir,' the salesperson explained. 'Nice and secure at the waist.' Ha, secure! The guy had no idea what he was talking about, but we'll get to that story. VK also reluctantly got himself a pair of walking shoes and I walked off with a pair too.

On Amar's advice, we bought a couple of umbrellas, though VK looked askance at my fivefold umbrella. 'Useless,' he declared. 'It's fivefold now, but will become sixfold at the slightest threat of rain and wind.'

'But it'll fit into any bag,' I countered, pleased with my reasoning and purchase. VK decided on a solid twofold one with a curved handle that would surely take up half the space in his briefcase. I felt more pleased.

As for bags, the salesperson displayed suitcases that he claimed would be perfect to carry the twenty-three kilos allowed by the airlines. 'I worked as ground staff at the airport,' he added.

'What if we packed them with huge stones?' I wanted to ask, just to disprove his confident claim. I didn't, of course, and, taking his advice, we bought four solid-looking, decent suitcases in pastel shades. VK turned down with horror my suggestion that we should go for bright colours since they'd be easy to spot. 'Orange, purple, neon green, turquoise, magenta...' He didn't even let me complete my list. 'We'll lose all our friends,' he said.

There was something VK purchased last minute, and that was a pen torch. Robin Jeffrey, a close friend, historian and writer who had recently been to Boston for the release of his latest book, *Waste of a Nation: Garbage and Growth in India*, co-authored by Assa Doron, mailed us tips on how to prepare for our trip. It was bitterly cold there, he wrote, and Syracuse was probably more of a Shivercurse, though the weather would improve by the time we got there. Among the things he advised us to take along was a pen torch. VK was a little taken aback. 'We are going to one of the most advanced nations in the world and Robin wants us to take a pen torch!' he commented, but bought one all the same, and tucked it into his tote bag. And throughout the trip we remained grateful to Robin for this invaluable suggestion.

A trip to the doctors' remained, since one of VK's key reasons for not venturing abroad was his asthma. Air conditioning never agrees with him and he would chuckle morbidly, to my uneasy distaste, that his destination at the end of a long flight would be a mobile mortuary. But his pulmonologist, Dr Arjun, who was also his former student, checked his lung capacity and brushed his fears out of the consultation room's window. 'You're fine and you'll have no problem, sir. In fact, you'll be better off there than here—purer air and all that. Just keep yourself well protected from the cold wind, and your trip will go like a breeze.'

Finally, we went for a routine check-up and the GP, Dr Krishna Kumar, certified us healthy to travel. So, we just took along the usual over-the-counter routine medicines that generally form part of travel paraphernalia. But, alas. There was one notable omission. More on that later.

Now that there was no going back, VK confessed there were a couple of things in the U.S. that had always stirred his interest. One was Walden Pond, dear to him because of his deep admiration for H.D. Thoreau, the American naturalist, environmentalist and abolitionist, and his even deeper admiration for E.O. Wilson, the American biologist and naturalist who held Thoreau in high esteem. The other thing he was interested in was the Boston Whale Watch. Since both were in Massachusetts, a visit to that American state became a must. And slowly a rough itinerary of our trip began to take shape. Amar, in consultation with Abdul Nizar, a very close friend in California who had been inviting us to the U.S. for years, began chalking up the plans.

# Night Flight to Dubai

WHY DO FLIGHTS FROM Thiruvananthapuram to other countries start at unearthly hours? A decent 2 p.m. flight would have been perfect, but no, the sadists who plan flight timings are determined to ensure sleepless nights for passengers. They must have very good reasons for this, but I'd like to imagine they are in league with pharmaceutical companies that manufacture sleeping pills.

Rajesh, VK's cousin, dropped us at the Thiruvananthapuram International Airport at 1 a.m. and we went in, feeling very international. Our flight to Dubai was at 4.35 a.m., but we had to report three hours in advance, and, clearing security and customs without any problem, we made our way to the boarding gate with a lot of time on our hands.

I've had heart-stopping experiences at airports—bags that beeped at security checks, trolleys that crashed into people and, on a couple of occasions, even ran over the toes of gentle Jekyll passengers who hopped in pain and turned instantly into ferocious Mr Hydes. I have waited at the wrong gate and sprinted to the right one just in time to hear my name being called one last time, while VK once forgot to collect his briefcase after the security check, discovering his oversight only when the cabin doors closed...

As I proceeded, relieved it had been smooth sailing this time, I noticed that VK, who generally marches ahead, was walking in a very peculiar manner. In fact, he wasn't walking as much as jerking, twisting and hopping along. Had he thrown his inhibitions to the winds because we were going to the U.S.? He appeared to be trying out some innovative break dance steps and moonwalk moves that might have raised Michael Jackson's shapely eyebrows. He stopped when he reached an empty seat and I rushed to him. 'Are you all right?' I asked.

'I'm all right,' he snapped, putting the briefcase down and letting go of the handle that had pulled his small suitcase along. 'It's these new jeans that aren't. They are slipping down.' He yanked them up almost to his chest.

'But how is that possible? The salesperson explained that the elastic...'

'Don't mention that guy,' he growled, hands still on the waistband of his jeans. He took a deep breath and continued, 'The wretched elastic is the villain. Tell me, how can you walk like a normal human being when you are holding a briefcase in your left hand, balancing a sling bag on that shoulder, dragging a suitcase with the other hand which also has a coat draped over the arm, and find that the weight of your phone is pulling down your jeans, thanks to the stupid elastic that stretches with every step I take?' Fire was threatening to come out of his nostrils.

Suppressing a giggle, I suggested he use a belt. 'Belt? I hate belts. Nothing but trouble. I deliberately left mine behind. I'd have to take it off at security checks, I...'

'Without it, your jeans will be at your feet and the security staff will haul you off for indecent exposure. You have to get one.'

At that moment, Amar called to ask if we were done with security and customs. 'All done, but these jeans have undone me,' I heard VK tell him. When the conversation was over, VK turned to me and said, 'I'm going to look for a belt here. Amar says it won't be easy to get them there, especially if you need to punch a hole or two in them.' VK's hourglass figure always calls for the punching of extra holes. He finally managed to buy a belt at the airport. He paid through his nose but it fitted around his waist. He still has it.

The sleek Emirates Boeing 777 stood against the midnight blue sky on the runway like a magnificent bird all poised for flight. Or it must have, but we didn't see it, for we used the aerobridge to stumble our bleary-eyed way into the plane. Two flight attendants, looking immaculate in their uniform familiarised by TV ads, welcomed us, their bright red lips breaking into wide smiles as if we were the right pair of long-lost twins they had been searching for. In their mushroom-coloured skirts and jackets topped with pert red caps sitting jauntily on their well-groomed heads, the tucked in white scarf flowing down to drape their shoulders, they looked so fresh I thought I must be dreaming. How can anyone look so bright, well-turned out and cheerful at 4 in the morning? A bit much.

Jolted into wakefulness by the million watt smiles, VK gave our seat numbers and one of them said, 'At the back.' We knew that; we had paid good money for those seats.

We found them and I settled down. VK took some time, though, for he didn't know what to do with the huge coat Amar insisted he carry with him during the flight. First, he put it on his lap, but it sat like a paperweight on him, pinning him down. Next, he rolled it and sat on it only to get the feel of sitting on a camel. He tried draping it over the armrest, but it kept slipping down. I would have loved to take bets on where it would fall—into the seat or outside. Finally, he went for the simplest solution—he wore it. I was already in my sweater, foolishly confident it would provide enough protection from the cold inside the plane.

The announcements were made and very soon the plane began to taxi. It took off for Dubai at exactly 4.35 a.m. We roared, soared and soon blended into the sky. I looked around, pleased to see an almost full flight. It is the same joy I experience when we are in a movie theatre that is houseful. It's a special feeling, to know that so many others are enjoying something with you, or sharing your headache if the movie is horrendous.

Very soon, a flight attendant, now minus the jacket, cap and scarf, but with the red smile still in place, came around, handing out small pouches that contained earplugs, eye masks and wet napkins. Thin blankets had already been provided. I had done my homework to prepare for the flight. To bypass jetlag, a friend who was a seasoned traveller said I should sleep throughout the flight, a piece of advice totally after my heart. I love such simple solutions. At the same time, she also asked me to walk occasionally, and I don't think she had sleep walking in mind.

Such contradictory advice was baffling until she

explained that walking was to prevent thrombosis from setting in. 'Keep moving your feet when you aren't walking,' she added. I got her drift, confusing as it may have been, but I'm glad she is not a commander in the army. What she meant was, try to sleep most of the time. For the rest, when you aren't walking but seated, move your feet in arcs, clockwise and anti-clockwise. Those people who have the irritating habit of shaking their legs all the time are well-equipped for safe air travel.

'Keep eating,' was another excellent recommendation. We were perfectly positioned for that. Our two seats being rather close to the back, we had easy and quick access to the galley. Galley, by the way, is the kitchen section on an aircraft. I took some time to figure it out when I first heard the word, for the diet of medieval adventure fiction in my childhood brought to my mind the low, narrow ships rowed by slaves. Our seats were close to the toilet too (you have to take the rough with the smooth) but not so close as to be smelly or have people perch on our shoulders like Sinbad the sailor to take brief bouts of rest as they queued up to go there.

At some point, it became very cold. VK, in his warm coat, was fine, while I wrapped the blanket around me. I still managed an enviable string of sneezes, much to the alarm of co-passengers seated close by, even in those healthy, pre-Covid times. If it were now, the plane would have emptied itself through the emergency doors.

One of the ways in which VK occupies himself while on an aircraft is to get a window seat and literally watch the world go by. But that didn't quite happen on the flight to Dubai. The early part was when it was still dark; so he, like everyone else on board, slept off, or at least tried to. When he woke up, he was not allowed to raise the shade. It was bright outside but most of the passengers were still asleep. Even the movie addicts seemed to have switched off their screens and were slumbering in positions their waking selves would have been embarrassed by.

I used the loo, but just as VK got ready to do so, the 'fasten your seatbelts' sign came on. An hour and a half remained of the journey to Dubai, but it did not change. And thus, we reached Dubai airport. We had to set our watches back by an hour and a half, and that was the beginning of this constant fiddling with our watches during the whole duration of our trip to the U.S., what with all those confusing time zones.

Dubai international airport was a shopping mall disguised as an airport. 'It's "Do buy" not "Dubai"', my nephew had once quipped, and the pun wasn't far off the mark. Hundreds of passengers yawned their way through the concourses, dragging suitcases and bags, and trying not to crash into branded exhibits with price tags that would have made our eyes roll if we hadn't been trying hard to keep them open. Dubai was the hub a lot of spokes connected to, and it looked like a lot of spokes were arriving in this hub in the morning.

# Chicago Ho!

WE BEGAN OUR LONG WALK to our next port of call—the gate for the flight to Chicago.

Security and other checks always made us nervous and the fact that we did not have much time to find the right terminal for the onward flight made us more anxious. Luckily, before we had disembarked, the screens on board showed a list of gates to head towards if we were taking a connecting flight and the Chicago flight was one of them.

We noticed there were arrows to help us move in the right direction, and we diligently followed them, walking on and on and on. VK remarked that at this rate, we would soon reach Abu Dhabi. We went gamely forward, while also keeping an eye out for—you guessed it—a washroom. VK located one, but gave up the idea of using it because of the length of the queue outside it. Like outside a liquor store in Kerala, he said, only with more diversity in styles of clothes and skin pigmentation. Afraid we'd be late at our check-in counter, we marched on. An announcement giving the gate number for passengers going to Chicago made us change our pace to a spirited trot.

What a relief to finally breast the tape at this finish.

People were already checking in and we joined two queues for security and immigration, armed with our papers and ready to answer any question we might be asked. 'Be prepared,' we had been told, for questions such as, 'Why are you going to the States?' 'What is your son's address?' 'When will you return and do you have your return tickets with you?' 'Do you have a prescription for these medicines or are you planning to run a pharmacy in America?' 'Did you not read the instructions about not carrying food in your luggage?'

Instead, why don't they ask meaningful questions like, 'Would you like to use the bathroom, sir?' 'Are you looking like something the cat dragged in because you ate an untimely meal, had a disturbed sleep and would like nothing better than to lie down in a quiet corner, or is this how you always look, ma'am?'

Why, we wondered, did different airports have different rules about cell phones, laptops, wallets, belts, handbags and other things people take with them? Manoj Dharmarajan, a good friend who is a worldly-wise travel veteran, having visited more than fifty countries, once told us that the only thing constant in international travel is the unpredictability and cussedness of immigration officials. But we were through without much fuss, maintaining eye contact even while in separate queues for security check, and otherwise keeping an eye on each other. Neither knew what to do, but we managed with our spirits, bodies and wallets intact.

The immigration process took place at the gate to board the flight to Chicago. There were separate queues for ladies and gents. The gents got away lightly, my gent did, at any rate.

VK's passage through immigration, manned by uniformed men and women, was pretty quick. He later said that he was mentally rehearsing, '740, E Shady Lane, Neenah, Wisconsin' and 'Software engineer, Kimberly Clark' so much, he might have mixed it up and said something like, 'Engineer Clark', 'Shady software', 'Neenah Lane' if he had been asked Amar's address, profession or the name of his company. Thankfully, no such questions were asked. He didn't even have to take off his shoes.

From a short distance, he watched a stern woman order me to remove my footwear. I did that and waggled my toes for good measure. Satisfied, though a trifle disappointed I hadn't stuffed dynamite into my socks, she proceeded to examine my bags and went through every single item in them. She gave a curt, unsmiling nod—the signal that I had been cleared—and turned her grim attention to the next person. I gathered my belongings and my self-respect, and joined VK.

We sat down, relieved the formalities were over, only to have VK jump up, reminded of what had been weighing on his mind and bladder. He rushed off to seek a toilet and returned very soon, for, hold your breath—no, not because of the smell—there was no toilet anywhere. Can you believe it? We couldn't, so I went with him to help him spot one, just in case, it being Dubai, it had been masquerading as a glitzy shop. But, no, there really wasn't a washroom around. I have never come across this deficiency at any other airport gate. And in Dubai, of all places, which seems to have everything else. We couldn't go outside the immigration area either. The only exit out of the place was into our plane.

'Control, control,' I whispered to VK as he sat cross-legged, looking mutinous. At last, the flight was announced and we boarded another Emirates 777 flight. The duo at the door went through the motions of welcoming us, made familiar by the earlier Emirates experience, except that the flight attendants this time were tall and strapping women.

We headed to our double seater at the back and settled down, as the flight attendants, who looked like East European basketball players, stomped up and down the aisle, as if keeping an alert eye for the right pass to score a basket.

This time we flew out in bright sunshine. VK sat by the window and had his nose stuck to the glass in his eagerness not to miss anything that flashed past. Very soon, he was peering down below, occasionally bending down so I could crane my neck and get a glimpse of features we had never seen before—desert, urban clusters and complexes of buildings surrounded by desert, roads, more desert and some more desert.

But he had an eye on the seatbelt sign too. It just would not go off. After an hour and a half, during which he must have wondered if there was a link between nephrologists and airline pilots, he got up and accosted a gargantuan airhostess at the back. I saw her give a wide grin, shake her head and point to the seatbelt sign that was still on. She said something too, probably, 'Oh, you lucky man, you might score a basket, if you are patient.' He returned, a grim look on his face and walked past our seats, all the way to the toilet in front. He was stopped from entering by another gigantic figure, the purser herself, this time. This aggressive point guard, wearing a cool, I-cannot-understand-such-a-need look on her face, said something to him. He replied, moved past her and went in, leaving her staring at the door.

When he returned, looking a little like Peter Sellers in the film *The Party*, I asked him what magic he had worked to get past the lady. He said she had protested that the captain didn't want anyone to leave the seats, but he had countered that his need was greater than the captain's command and he would take responsibility for any problems that might arise because of his noncompliance.

And while on the subject, he went on about what he thought was wrong with the design team of aircrafts and terminals. The team should also include anatomists who know about the capacity of the human bladder and some statistically smart, medically aware engineer-MBA types who can provide inputs on human outputs, so to speak, so that the necessary conveniences are in place before they hustle a few hundred people into a flying aluminium tube or several thousand into terminals, he snorted.

Having got this off his chest, he settled down to watch the world below. I twiddled with the buttons on the seatback screen for a bit before switching it and myself off. As in-flight entertainment, VK chose the screen that gave a constant view of the map of the world and tracked our flight. The map did not indicate political divisions; one had to make inspired guesses. Were we flying over Iraq or Iran? He wasn't sure, he later said, but at one point he saw what appeared to be military vehicles—semi-destroyed ones—against a desert background. Soon after, mountain ranges, with and without snow, were clearly visible.

The entire flight was in daylight, so meal and sleep times didn't sync with the body, though we never said no to any meal provided. Even looking out of the window needed some energy. In between bouts of sleep, VK watched parts of Russia and, perhaps, Scandinavia, missed all of the North Atlantic or, at least, the seas north of the Atlantic, but woke up to look down on ice and snow and more of it over Greenland and all the way to the Canadian airspace. And they appeared in so many different patterns. So much of white, arranged in diverse ways.

As for me, I stuck to my plan of sleep, walk, eat. Curling up as comfortably as an economy class seat would allow, I focussed on sleeping as much as possible. There was a guy in front who was absorbing drinks like a sponge and I kept a close watch on him while awake, hoping for some entertainment, but alas. He had a very simple plan up his gullet—drink, drink, sleep, sleep, drink, drink—and he stuck to it.

I managed a few walks too. After an ambitious walk along all the aisles that stressed me out, trying to dodge the human impediments, some of them carrying laden trays, I decided to limit myself to walks to the galley and the occasional one to the loo. The galley was well stocked with chocolates, fruits, nuts and drinks. Not a fan of soft drinks, I would go for water, the good old Adam's ale, and return to my seat with some fruits, nuts or chocolate. VK would take some nuts and go back to peering down the glass window while I'd move my feet, chomp on the fruits, and then curl up again.

Under the watchful eyes of VK, the green and brown

of soil and vegetation gradually began to appear along with the white of snow and ice. Soon the green and brown took over completely, to be followed by buildings, roads and all the signs of being near a big city. VK woke me up. I strained my eyes, hoping to see the intricate criss-crosses of runways and taxiways I had seen in aerial view pictures of O'Hare airport, but before I knew what was happening, the plane had landed and, bumping along, we observed instead, sights familiar at most big airports in India—other aircraft and vehicles, mostly tractors towing luggage or equipment or taking men one way or the other. But there was one difference—there was a striking mix of colour and ethnicity. This was the U.S.

It was 3 p.m. on 27 April when we landed in O'Hare International Airport, Chicago. Time had turned on its head. Aha, so this was what caused the jet lag people who travelled abroad talked about, though I never could quite understand it. Well, to be honest, I never tried to find out but always politely asked people who had travelled, even from Colombo, 'How's your jet lag?'

Once the doors opened, the plane emptied itself, in order and in silence, with passengers patiently waiting their turn to get up and collect the baggage from the overhead bin before moving forward. What a refreshing contrast to what happens in India, where the moment the plane touches down, you hear the clicking of seat belts being unfastened, followed by passengers jumping up, and then being cautioned by harried air hostesses. They sit down as if on pins, ready to leap up as soon as the plane comes to a standstill, and, then, stand poised on one foot, giving the impression they would love to shove their way to the exit doors if they could.

The flight attendants bid us cheery goodbyes, appearing obscenely fresh, while we mumbled pleasantries in response, looking as if we had been churned without detergents in a washing machine. As we came through the gate, I changed the time on my watch once again. I wasn't able to linger for a bit and savour the special, 'I'm actually standing on U.S. asphalt' moment, for we had to keep the other passengers in sight. I had learnt through experience that the best thing to do after landing in a strange airport is to follow the crowd to know where to head next, or at least pick a sensible-looking duo and trail them. They could end up leading you to the washroom, but that's a risk you have to take.

We had been told we'd take a long time getting through immigration and that was no exaggeration. We were led by the crowd to the CBP (Custom and Border Protection) Processing Area and there we stopped short, all at sea in an airport. Everyone but us seemed to know what to do as they headed for machines that we later came to know were APC—Automatic Passport Control—kiosks. We'd come into a country where self-help and machine help were considered the best help. There were volunteers around with 'We Can Help You' on the backs of their t-shirts, but when we approached an enthusiastic guy who had just finished assisting a blonde, he waved us towards a machine and went to the next attractive young thing. They should change the text to, 'We can help you—if you are young, female, and blonde,' I thought to myself.

VK watched the actions of others, then ventured, very

cautiously, to follow suit and succeeded in getting the required receipts. We had been given forms to fill on the plane. We added those to the receipts and joined the tourist visa queue. The rest was very easy and once we collected our baggage, we headed to the exit lounge. The airport was warm and lulled us into a false sense of comfort, so much so that VK took off his coat before setting to work to insert the new SIM into his phone, and, voilà; it worked.

# Chicago

THE FIRST CALL VK MADE from the new SIM was to his son who said he was fifteen minutes away. We were to wait outside; he'd arrive shortly. With great joy, we wheeled our trolleys out, only to be welcomed with a huge blast of freezing cold air. Brrrrrr. It was windy Chicago all right. VK quickly donned his coat. I had a lot of warm clothes, all safe in our suitcases. We stood there, shivering, our teeth chattering, our numb hands hardly able to grip our bags.

A car drew up, and, recognising Amar, we rushed to it. We must have been going blue with cold for he leaped out, took one look at us and asked us to get into the car; he'd take care of the luggage. 'Quick, I've turned up the heater,' he said. VK jumped in and jumped out immediately for he had leaped into the driver's seat. This was the U.S. and, on their roads, left was right and right was left. It took us a few days to get this right.

As we sat in the car, thawing slowly, Amar put the luggage into the dickey—trunk in American English—and we were off into the streets of Chicago. De-frozen, we were now able to gape at Chicago's famed skyline. The rectangular boxes were all over the place; it was truly the land of the skyscraper. It was a strange feeling, to be hemmed in by high rises all around, and I felt a trifle claustrophobic.

On our way to the hotel, Amar began educating us about driving in the U.S. He explained how, at minor junctions, drivers followed a zip system to decide whose turn it was to enter a fork. One car from one road moved ahead. The car behind drew up to where the first had been parked but did not follow the car in front. A car from the other fork now had its turn; followed by one from the first road. It seemed to work very well. No honking, no snarling, no pushing ahead of your turn. In fact, we heard the sound of a car honk only twice during our entire U.S. trip, and both times when I tried out the horn on a friend's car.

What a far cry from Indian roads where honking is a compulsion, and happens even if there is only one car on the road. If you have a car, you must toot your horn and let the whole world know, is the philosophy that drives a driver in India. In unsupervised junctions or forks on the road, it is a free for all and the most daring driver wins. But, one has to admit, it is a sort of functioning chaos.

The discipline of drivers in the U.S. was impressive. We noticed very few policemen around. At junctions with traffic signals, the signs were respected and everyone waited their turn. Cars were only too happy to stop for pedestrians who could press a button on a post and claim the right to walk across. No one threatened to mow them down. In fact, drivers in cars reacted as if they'd like to lay down the red carpet for pedestrians if that were possible.

Post this tutoring about roads in the U.S., we reached Candlewood Suites, a cosy, warm place where Amar had booked a suite. While we freshened up, Amar, not too familiar with Chicago, located an Indian restaurant and we soon headed there for dinner. Eager for my first visit to a restaurant in the U.S., I had one impatient foot inside the door when Amar pulled me back. 'No, wait,' he warned. It was time for my first lesson on restaurant etiquette in the U.S.

'Whether it is Indian, American, Thai or Greek, you don't walk in and pick your seat—near the window, far away from the wash room,' he tutored me. 'You have to wait at the entrance and catch the eye of someone who works in the restaurant, who then comes over.'

'Oh, okay.' This was quite unlike India where you can just barge into a restaurant. If it's full, you take a quick look around, and make straight for the table where people are having their dessert and plant yourself next to them, sending silent but strong signals, until they choke over the fruit salad, pay the bill and vamoose.

We waited, and soon a jaunty young chap greeted us with an enthusiastic, 'Hi! How are you doing? May I help you?'

'Hi. Table for three, please,' my son said.

I was thrilled by the profuse welcome. My charm was already working. 'Hi,' I began, smiling broadly. 'I'm doing fine, thank you very much. And...'

But the chap had turned his complete attention to a couple standing behind us. 'Hi. How are you doing?' He addressed them.

I learnt soon enough that this was standard American courtesy. Wherever you go, whether it is a shop, a restaurant, a billing counter or a bus station, you are greeted with a bright 'Hi' or a delighted 'Hello' accompanied by a brilliant smile that immediately fades and reappears like a flash to welcome the person behind you.

Another chap soon arrived and led us like meek lambs to the table. Amar said you could express a preference for another table and they would oblige, but hardly anyone did that. We gave our order—parathas, roti and a mughlai curry for Amar and me, and chicken biryani for VK. We ate rather silently; I wasn't sure if we could talk while eating. What if someone strode to our table to say with a grin, 'Hi! How are you doing? Would you please leave the restaurant? We don't allow conversation here.'

As we tucked in, VK exclaimed, 'Ssh, ah, ha.'

'Ah ha, he likes the food,' I thought and smiled at Amar.

But soon it became clear that they weren't appreciative noises, but his palate's protests at the spicy food. When Amar saw him push the plate away with tears in his eyes, he said, 'I'll ask them to box it.'

Box it? I looked at him quizzically. 'You mean they'll spank the biryani, "Naughty, naughty", and throw it away? Haha!'

'Box means to parcel the food,' Amar laughed. 'They'll give us a cardboard box. We have to put the food in.' That made very good sense, I thought. We can scrape every morsel into the box. I always had this sneaking feeling that not all the food you asked to be parcelled went into the takeaway containers. Amar added that if you don't wish to eat at the table, you can place your order at the counter, and say you wish for something 'To go.' And you wait, get the box, and, well, go.

Amar paid the bill with his credit card which was swiped and returned, along with a receipt. 'What about the tip?' I asked. I had heard so much about the tipping culture in the U.S.

'This is the "tipping point",' Amar smiled. 'Look, here's the space on the receipt for the tip and you write the amount; 10 to 15 per cent of the bill amount is the normal tip. Pay 20 or 25 per cent and the waiter will add you in his prayers.' He booked himself a mention in our waiter's prayers with his 25 per cent tip. 'They don't take the card again. Since they have already swiped the card, they can simply include the tip amount.'

'Can't they add more than you have specified?' I asked.

He said, 'Well, I suppose they can but everything is based on trust and there is no hanky panky.'

No PIN or OTP required either. It's all very simple in the U.S. And therefore, not too safe and foolproof, but then the trust factor is pretty big. This amazing, trust-based system is available in India too these days, but I cannot imagine it working too well in my country, for some reason. Three or four dinners at swanky restaurants and, for all you know, a millionaire would be left counting their pennies.

'Waiters in the U.S. work for minimum wages and there's a kind of tacit understanding that they should earn the rest from tips,' Amar explained as we left the restaurant. 'They do earn a sizeable part of their money through tips. If they received living wages, that would be fine, but they don't; so, they look forward to a better life through tips.'

I looked forward to a good night's sleep. Returning to Candlewood Suites, we were settling down in our room, when Amar commented, looking a little anxious, 'I don't think you'll be able to sleep well tonight.'

'Sez who?' I retorted. Should it have been 'whom'? No, 'who'. Anyway, whom cares? I was already in deep slumber. All that sleeping, walking and eating during the flight had paid off.

⌣

'Let's walk around and scout for a restaurant for breakfast rather than rely on Google search,' Amar suggested the next morning.

'Yay,' I responded, all game for adventure. But it ended tamely, for we spotted an attractive one just down the road. This time I remembered to stand at the door and respond with just a smile at the extravagant greeting. We were led to a table near the window for a delightful view of the serene scene outside while, inside, the restaurant bustled with vibrant life—tables with people displaying various degrees of satisfaction depending on which stage of their breakfast they had reached, while smiling waiters hopped about.

'Pancakes,' I chose from the menu without a second thought. I had always wanted to eat authentic pancakes, though, when I was a child, I had been conned into believing that the pancake was actually our very own dosa. Here was my chance to discover how closely related the two were.

My choice was perfect—what delicious pancakes. They were everything I'd hoped they'd be, though I must confess I'd no idea what to hope for. Whether they originated in the Stone Age—a rough imitation of a primal pancake had been found in the stomach of Otzi the Iceman, but I wouldn't wish to taste that—or were invented by the Romans, the American version was just wow. And didn't justify the 'flat as a pancake' analogy, since I've seen flatter dosas.

I remembered an interesting titbit I had read regarding that popular phrase. In the early twenty-first century, three geologists, seeking some diversion during their dull excursion across the American Midwest, decided to find out the relative flatness of pancakes and Kansas through topographic profiling. They came out with the astonishing and gleeful discovery that Kansas was flatter. This flat state theory didn't amuse Kansas geographers, who, determined to defend the honour of their state but unable to disprove its flatness, found solace in comforting comparisons. They pointed out that while Kansas might be flatter than a pancake, other states like Florida and Illinois were even flatter.

Tucking into the flat pancake at a restaurant in the flatter state of Illinois, what pleased me most was the superlative taste.

The cheerful waiter placed a bottle of maple syrup close to my plate. I was a little wary of maple syrup. Prithvi, the cousin in Chennai, had paid a small fortune to get a bottle of imported maple syrup to celebrate his daughter's return from Paris after her studies. 'It tasted awful,' he had confessed, and now it sat like an ornament at the centre of his dining table, gazing superciliously down at the native pickle and homely sauce bottles.

But Amar encouraged me to have a go—it's the ideal combination with pancakes, he enthused. I took a cautious lick and gave up. I assumed it was an acquired taste, and I wouldn't have time to acquire the taste during the half hour it took to have breakfast.

For the first time, I witnessed first-hand the American obsession with size. When I saw the huge pancakes, my eyes turned as large as the non-existent saucer on the table, the coffee being served in mugs. Amar had ordered scrambled eggs and VK an omelette. The scrambled eggs came in a mountainous heap and the omelette almost overflowed from the huge plate. Obviously, the hard work of a lot of hens had gone into their preparation.

And then there were the mugs. Enormous jugs, almost, of coffee brought and placed on the table—drink coffee king size! I took a surreptitious glance around and found that no one else seemed to be intimidated by the giant coffee mugs—they were guzzling their coffee as if it were water. The moment I finished mine, the waiter refilled it. Aghast, I protested. For one, I had just finished drinking that monstrous quantity with great difficulty, for another I thought we'd have to pay for it, and I was beginning to be horrified at how expensive everything was in the U.S., when converting dollar into rupees, of course. Though Amar had warned us against that—it doesn't make sense, he said, and it would be a total killjoy—how could we not? One dollar is NOT one rupee, after all. By the end of the trip, I had become an expert at mental mathematics.

Apparently, you don't have to pay for the refilled coffee, but I'd gladly have refilled the waiter's coffeepot with some from my first mugful. Smacking his lips after a satisfying breakfast, VK announced that the huge size of everything put him off food. Ha!

Filled to the gullet with pancakes and eggs, and overflowing with coffee, it was only fitting that our next destination be something monumental—The Art Institute of Chicago, the second largest art museum in the U.S. Even as the two enormous statues of bronze lions, sculpted by Edward Kemeys, that flanked the entrance greeted us, looking rather stand-offish, a feeling of awe threatened to overwhelm us at the sheer size of the place.

The admission cost a tiny fortune, but the experience was well worth it. You could spend days there and still not see everything. That was the whole idea—woo people in, get them hooked and ensure multiple visits in future. We had to make our choice, and since the museum boasted of one of the best collections of paintings in the U.S., we went to the European Art Section that displayed the Impressionist and post-Impressionist paintings. They made a huge impression all right. We moaned with joy over the Monet collection, ran our eyes over Renoir's 'Two Sisters', gawked at Van Gogh's self-portrait, a pre-ear mutilation effort. Cézanne seized our attention with 'The Bathers' though 'Madame Cézanne in a Yellow Chair' looked grimly disapproving.

By this time, my hunger pangs began. I have a strange problem—the moment I check my watch and find it's close to meal time, I get hungry and must eat, great art or no art. VK gets lost in museums, and true to form, he was already living on love of artefacts and recycled air.

When I mentioned lunch, he looked as if I had made some vulgar suggestion. I appealed to my son, who was a neutral party—he could tilt towards VK's standpoint and go hungry for hours or could hear the rumbling of my stomach and take my side. Thankfully Amar had digested his scrambled eggs only too well and chose to come with me to forage for food. We followed the helpful arrows that led us to the museum canteen to find that lunch was from 12 to 2, and it was close to 2.

Most outlets there had already stopped serving and, looking desperately about us, we found an Indian place that had roti and Goan fish curry—creatively described, for there was only curry and no fish. After some earnest search in the curry with the wooden spoon provided, I fished out a disintegrated bit that had seen better days. We grabbed the two pieces of roti—the last on offer—and made our way to a table. With a great sense of timing, VK joined us. We sat down and shared the food among the three of us, not that it would have mattered to VK what he got, for he was in a hurry to head back to the art gallery. He wouldn't even have noticed if we had offered him the literature about the museum we had picked up at the entrance; he'd have chewed on it, wiped his lips, commented, 'Nice, tasty, tasty, nice,' and disappeared into the museum.

VK later said, rather apologetically, that this kind of disregard for food was mostly because he felt we could get food whenever we wanted; art was a rare commodity. So, sublime feelings for art and artefacts took precedence over pandering to baser instincts. Ah, but that's in India, I countered. Not in the U.S. which is so rule bound that if you are late, you don't get anything. In fact, as we later learnt, you have to get to the food counter 15 minutes before it closes, for at the exact time, the waitresses pull down the shutters, turn their butts to us and are halfway to the station to catch their train before you can say, 'Bread and butt....'

Corridors led to corridors and we cried halt only when Amar said we had another place to go. We did a last-minute scamper through Ancient Greece, Mesopotamia and Egypt, nodded at gods and goddesses, hobnobbed briefly with hallowed Greek philosophers, stared at exquisite pieces of pottery and artefacts, stepped back hastily from the mummies, smiled at the Buddha who beckoned from the 'Arts of Asia' collection and came out of the museum, with VK managing a crick in his neck as he kept turning back to give it long, lingering looks.

'To a skyscraper next,' said Amar, booking a cab on his phone. 'That one.' In the cab he pointed to a tall building in the distance that dwarfed other skyscrapers in the skyline. I got it. 'Ooh, Sears Tower?'

'No, Willis,' he said with a laugh. 'Same place. Name changed when it changed hands.' Of course, don't we know about re-naming places? It's a worldwide ploy to feed egos and keep people confused, but unwittingly helps their memories remain healthy and ticking.

At the time of our visit, the Willis Tower was the mother of all skyscrapers in the U.S., with One World Trade Center, which was higher, playing father. Standing tall and proud, its chief aim in life is to give short people a complex. And house more than a hundred businesses, of course. We joined a long queue of differently-hued people, lending it some more colour, and waited for ages. Finally, after clearing tight security checks at different points, we entered a big glass lift, sorry, elevator, and flew to the observation deck, called the

Skydeck, at the top, in 60 seconds flat, clipping a second or two from Batman's speed.

From the observation deck, we observed, marvelling at the fantastic view of the high-rise buildings that defined Chicago and felt a special thrill looking down on them. From the ledge, or the glass-boxed balcony, we could look right down and watch tiny toy cars make their way around the ribbon strips, also known as roads. The drizzle made the view a little hazier and more mysterious, adding to the fascination. It was like playing Lego in dim light.

# The Octopus is Not for Eating

GOING UP TO A HEIGHT of 1,353 feet can be pretty exhausting, even if it was an elevator that did all the hard work. We returned to Candlewood, tired but pleased. Amar's friend Ujjal, who was in Chicago, wanted to take us out for dinner at a Greek restaurant, and there we went. We found the restaurant bustling with people—a welcome change from the streets where you find only cars and hardly any humans on the pavements, sorry, sidewalks. Once again, we encountered huge portions. Just looking at the thick noodles and chicken I had ordered took care of my hunger. VK went for a chicken sandwich, Amar for spaghetti while Ujjal ordered a leg of lamb. After a whispered consultation with Amar, Ujjal added octopus to his order.

I stared with fascination at the dish when it arrived—Greek marinated octopus in oil and vinegar. The octopus's appendage curled on the plate like a well-fed little snake—the sight put me off. My primeval fear of snakes extended to lookalikes garnished with onions. Ujjal did the honours—he cut it with great panache and offered it to us. I refused outright, happy to offer my allergy to squid as an excuse. I declared I didn't wish to take a chance with its cousin.

VK, on the other hand, a conservative eater who is always happy with the dish he's ordered—mostly noodles—actually nodded his head to say 'yes'. I was shocked. 'Are you going to eat OC-TO-PUS?' I asked, sounding suitably bewildered. He who says no to squid, frowns at crab and turns away from oyster, now nods his head like an eager schoolboy and wishes to eat octopus? How could one explain this?

'Yes, I'll taste it,' he nodded once again, an adventurous gleam in his eyes. Ujjal placed two small slices on VK's plate before he and Amar proceeded to serve themselves generously from the dish. I soon noticed that VK, who had been waxing eloquent pre-octopus, had become silent. Now, I've heard that octopus meat is a delicacy. He was relishing the taste, I thought, a little envious. Savouring it slowly, giving it his complete attention. And I wasn't wrong, for he was—in a way. He turned to me and whispered he had blisters in his mouth.

Blisters? How could blisters develop so quickly? 'The mayonnaise!' I exclaimed, worried. I recalled his adverse reaction to mayonnaise on a couple of occasions. The starters had come with a dash of mayonnaise. He should've avoided those. Or maybe the giant sandwich was the culprit. I alerted the others and we gave unsolicited advice while VK sat there, looking sick. 'Don't touch the starters.' 'Stop eating the sandwich.' 'Spit out the oct...' We looked at one another with a wild surmise. 'Yus. It must be the octopus,' we chorused. VK's lips had now become thick. It was clearly an allergic reaction to something. He stopped eating but signalled that we carry on. I stopped too. The other two paid scant justice to the food. We decided to call it a night. VK thanked Ujjal, reassuring him through ballooning lips that he was fine and would sleep this off. We returned to Candlewood, the food boxed. Ujjal took the boxed octopus. When we last heard, he, Ujjal, I mean, was hale and hearty.

We found we hadn't brought along any anti-allergy medicine—an unfortunate omission. Amar hovered around, looking anxious till VK insisted he was okay and asked him to get some well-deserved rest—he had had a long day. Amar went off to make his bed on the living room sofa and lie on it. VK wanted to turn in and I was relieved, thinking the rest would do him good. But after some tossing and turning, he held his stomach and demanded an antacid. I gave him a tablet, but that didn't help. A little later he threw up ... and threw up ... and threw up. I was reminded of the limerick about the young lady from Spain, who got sick as she rode on a train. Not once, but again. And again, and again, and again and again and again. I was amazed at the quantity he brought up. There was no co-relation between input and output.

This time I was on surer ground for I had the medicine for putting a stop to vomiting. VK's stomach settled after he took the pill, but he was totally exhausted and soon was fast asleep. I lay awake for some time, relieved and at the same time, worried. This was only our second full day in the U.S. How were we going to survive the rest of the trip? But one thing was certain—there was never going to be any love lost between VK and the octopus.

Amar, meanwhile, tired out after all that driving, slept through this entire drama and light and sound effect. He couldn't believe he had slept better than a log when we updated him the next morning. VK woke up still feeling drained but much better. We checked out at 10.30 a.m.

We were on the road again. VK had had only chocolates for breakfast—he said he was planning on going without food for a day, to settle his stomach, chocolates not counting as proper food, merely energy providers. I soon realised that Amar was also planning to keep his father company and stay hungry for there had been no mention of breakfast when we checked out and now we were driving from Chicago to Neenah. Hunger pangs began the moment I realised this but I decided to wait stoically till I was close to fainting.

# On the Way to Neenah

THE DISTANCE FROM CHICAGO TO Neenah is about three hundred kilometres and takes about three hours by road. Amar was not trying to set any land speed record; in fact he wanted us to enjoy the sights, so we took a little longer. Two things about the drive stand out in my memory—how spotlessly clean the whole place appeared to be, and how few people there were about.

As we were making our way through Chicago to Interstate 41 that would take us to Neenah, I noticed a few big sheets of paper and some trash under a bridge. Trash. I was ecstatic. This was the first time, since we'd landed, that I was seeing any litter. Amar explained that a vagrant must have slept rough there the previous night and not bothered to remove his makeshift mattress. Yes, the U.S. has its homeless too; a sobering thought.

Meanwhile I decided to cry halt to my martyr act and declared I was hungry. 'Don't even mention food; I'll throw up,' VK protested.

I decided I wouldn't and whispered to Amar, 'How about some delayed breakfast somewhere?' Poor guy, he too had probably been hoping I'd take the initiative for he swiftly pulled over at an Oasis outlet on the highway over the Illinois Tollway. We bought sandwiches, monster ones, of course, and munched on them, out of the sight of VK who remained in the car. Satiated, we were soon tootling along again.

An extraordinary thing I noticed was the absence of people. There was no one on the pavements, or indeed the lawns and yards and fields that were visible. Where were all the people? Inside cars, of course. There was a never-ending procession of cars and other four-wheelers, and we could spot faces in the vehicles that we passed or those that thundered past; often truck drivers intent on their job of taking consignment X to place Y as efficiently as possible. We did see one body attached to a face when a flamboyant Harley Davidson rider overtook us—we were driving through Harley Davidson country and were excited when Amar pointed out their factory.

During the whole journey we saw only two people actually walking. I'm not kidding. A woman and a man. Separately. The woman, in blue jeans and boots, walked briskly along what appeared to be an endless lawn before an invisible house. The man we caught walking, appeared to be doing nothing. He had to be a philosopher, I thought.

This remained our experience whether it was on our bus ride from New York to Boston, the rail journeys we took or the long drives in California. So much land, so many cars, so few people. No wonder the Mexicans are trudging in.

We drove a lot around the Midwest. The amount of grass being trimmed by men riding lawn mowers was unbelievable. No blade of grass in America, it appeared, had the right to grow beyond an inch or two. A minor transgression and it would be promptly cut to size by a human on a lawn mower the size of a small car in India. Where were all the cows that could have grazed on all this grass, I wondered. We had passed several dairies, identifiable because of boards that said so. The cows, like the people, were not to be seen. Not even driving cars.

The contrast with my native land was striking. Though our highways are now beginning to resemble ones we see in foreign cities, you cannot drive in India, look out the window and not spot people. Or litter. Or, I imagine, in some parts of India, cows.

Around lunch time, Amar stopped at a place called Nutrition Café. VK, now on a steady diet of chocolates, decided he wasn't game to change it yet. He opted to remain outside the restaurant and stretch his legs. I walked about with him for a bit while Amar parked the car. The car park here was as neat and as stylishly laid out as the one at Candlewood and the other parts of Chicago we had visited.

'American bricklayers are meticulous and artistic all right,' VK remarked approvingly. 'Look at the symmetry of all this brickwork.' There was, however, a dirty white mound on one corner of the parking yard that appeared to beckon us. On getting close we realised it was snow. I circled it, kicked it and touched it. It took all the abuse stoically. I think it must have been craving attention.

There were trees planted in neat lines in the park and some of them had a deep reddish covering of very tender leaves. 'I've seen similar trees in Chicago,' VK observed. Leaving him to muse over the leaves, the trees, their name and origin, I followed Amar into the restaurant.

We returned to find VK in conversation with a young chap, balanced on a cycle. VK later said that when he saw this guy cycle up and stop under a window, he went up to him and greeted him. No response. When he helloed a third time, the chap pulled a pair of ear phones out of his ears and smiled. VK asked him the name of the trees. He had no idea, and wanted to know if VK had the answer. VK told him he had been in the country less than 48 hours and was clueless.

Soon they got talking. The nameless chap had just finished high school and had gained admission to a degree course at the University of Wisconsin, Madison. He would soon be leaving to pursue it. He seemed very excited at the prospect. He had picked his course that combined climate science and agriculture with care for he wanted to become a consultant to big farms. There was a lot of money in it, he said.

I was just in time to hear him emphasise that he wanted to make money. 'Lots and lots of money.'

'We're in the U.S. to attend the graduation ceremony of our daughter-in-law who has just finished an MS in Information Management at Syracuse,' VK volunteered. I thought he puffed up a little.

The guy must have been impressed because he drawled, 'Aw, really?' and punctuated it with a series of 'wows'. Half were, presumably, for the university and half for the course.

VK hadn't finished with him yet. 'What exactly will you do as a consultant? I've not heard of an agriculturalist whose focus is the climate.'

'With cloud computing, AI, advanced satellite networks and so on,' the youth explained, 'it would be possible to give clients, big farmers, very specific weather predictions and other hints on how to run their farms more efficiently.'

Farmers would, in the future, need such information and he would, in a few years, be ready to provide it. This proved what we already knew even before going to the States. The American universities are so good because they are very quick and responsive to the changing world. Half the country and the then president thought that climate change was a hoax or a problem that would take care of itself. And here, in a region that was conservative, was a famous university designing and offering a remarkable course, very much taking climate change into consideration. And young people, like this chap talking to us, were enthusiastically pursuing it.

At this point, the window slid open and a woman's head popped out. She offered him a packet. He had been lingering near the window because it was where cars drove up and drivers ordered food still seated in their cars. As he bid goodbye, VK asked, 'How far are we from Neenah?'

'This is Neenah.' He grinned, waved and zoomed off, bent over his handle bars like a racer.

That was a cheery welcome, and a refreshing change from the cold, curt one to the country itself at O'Hare airport. This chance meeting with young American blood warmed our hearts all right. VK learned later, at the FDR Memorial at Fishkill, that the tree was the Japanese maple, to be distinguished from the native maple. A well-informed guide at that museum who enlightened VK on this, made his day when he also volunteered more detailed information about the tree.

# Neenah

AMAR STOPPED AT NEENAH'S GIANT Walmart Supercenter
on the way home. This was my first visit to any Walmart
outlet—in fact, it was my first experience of an American
supermarket—and it was super impressive all right. You
could play football there; it was so huge, but then the size
of anything in America had ceased to surprise. The variety
of items on offer, though, was mind-boggling and we felt
almost apologetic about buying only a couple of loaves of
bread, milk and eggs, and not a truckload of stuff. Though
even the simple act of picking up a loaf of bread took on
metaphysical hues—there were loaves of all sizes, colour and
combination of ingredients on display. Finally, I solved the
problem by asking Amar to pick up his normal choice and
get the milk and eggs too. What if I had to select milk that
came from different varieties of cows and eggs based on the
pedigree of the hens' ancestors?

Amar took our purchase to a checkout counter and I
watched, intrigued, as he scanned the items and made the
payment, totally unsupervised, before putting the stuff into
a bag. He had gone for the self-checkout option and I came
up with the inevitable 'What if?' Coming from India, where

a small section of the population always looks for ingenious non-paying options, I couldn't help but ask. 'No way,' Amar responded, as we walked towards the parking area. 'There will be a beep to alert the staff.' Of course. I should have guessed that the tech watchdog would be on it.

We reached Amar's apartment by 3.30 p.m. It was on the first floor—we had to climb a flight of steep rug-covered steps and I banged into the door by tripping over the last. Amar quickly unlocked it and I stumbled in. The living room looked so neat, cosy and welcoming, I dived into the capacious sofa that was the first piece of furniture to meet my eyes.

How was I to know the sofa had the softest foam stuffing possible? I just sank into its depths before Amar could warn me. Amar and VK had to yank me out by my feet. I soon learnt that one had to treat it like a trench bunker and slip in carefully for a comfortable seating position.

I checked the bathroom next. Indians know about the Western phobia for water in toilets and the mania for paper. I hoped for the convenience of a bidet shower but it was absent. However, to my huge relief, I found that my thoughtful son had kept a bucketful of water close by. I recalled the words of a friend of ours, Shashi Kumar, who had a son in the U.K. and a daughter in Australia. When they invited him to visit them, he said, 'Only if there's a bucket and a mug in the bathroom.'

Dinner came out of some of the boxes we had collected in the last couple of days—Amar and I had the parathas, roti and chicken from the Indian restaurant of the first day, while VK felt it was time to attempt eating something other than chocolates. He decided on bread, and—yes, you guessed right—chocolate. After dinner, we informed people at home we'd reached safely, and we went to bed. And a very comfortable bed it was too, without belonging to the sinking ilk. In no time we were lost to the world. Jet lag? What's that?

We woke up, feeling fine. I made coffee and served it in decent-sized mugs—Amar had a stock of them in different sizes, and tiny teacups too. The latter were rejected outright; those were for the Chinese and the Japanese. No prize for guessing what was for breakfast—omelettes to go with bread and butter. There was jam too; VK took a little of that but went easy on the butter.

I had noticed Amar sitting with his laptop and peering occasionally into books the previous night, and over breakfast I asked him what it was all about. He said he had applied for a new job, since his company, Cognizant, that he had been ultra-loyal to, never having jumped from it higher or sideways, had no openings for him in New York, where Arpitha had a position with Ernst and Young (E&Y). E&Y, meanwhile, didn't have anything suitable in Wisconsin for her. If they had to be together, one of them would have to move. Amar decided it would be him, since Arpitha had just landed her job. He had an interview that evening with the company Bed Bath & Beyond that appeared interested in hiring him. What, what and what? What a name.

'Are you sure you want to work there?' I asked, sounding suspicious.

Amar laughed. 'Not to worry; it's a reputed American retail store company,' he said, and left for work.

VK and I were relaxing when a constant humming sound in the background prompted me to investigate. Looking out the window of the bedroom, I saw a man riding on a lawn mower. The windows were closed to keep off the cold—Wisconsin was facing a delayed spring that year and the weather was still chilly—but the noise was audible in spite of that. While the kind of cacophonous noise familiar in India would never be found in the U.S., the American love for gadgets does bring a lot of noise into their life, and that of their neighbours'. The vacuum cleaner, lawn mower, snow or leaf blower are all America's gifts to ensure disturbed sleep.

I had seen a riding mower only in pictures and for a while I entertained myself watching the meticulous mower work its steady way through the lawn. The driver looked as if he was there just for the ride; I really couldn't find any difference to the lawn after the mower had passed over it, but then it was probably a millimetre of errant growth that was being clipped.

Setting speculation aside, I went to get lunch ready. This time it was food boxed after the memorable dinner at the Greek restaurant—no octopus, though. I punished myself by having those awful thick noodles that appeared to have grown fatter in the fridge. VK had bread again, with a chocolate—again. He christened this combination the American 'kanji and payaru'—rice gruel and lentils.

The noodles didn't agree with me—I seriously think that Greek restaurants should have a tummy upset alert pinned to the menu card—and I wanted to use the washroom just when VK had gone in for a bath. Amar had given us strict instructions not to open the bathroom door while bathing or after, till the steam had completely disappeared, else it'd set off the fire alarm. Arpitha had once invited a fire engine to their apartment just by having a warm bath. What an alarming country. As soon as VK strolled out asking for a towel, I flung it at him, practically hustled him out of the way and made it with a hop, skip and jump. I realised I should go easy on food here.

Amar returned at about 6. He said the interview was okay, not great. He had always been one for saying a standard 'okay' after his exams, from his school days, and I had learnt to interpret and slot his 'okays' from the tone. This 'okay' meant the Bed part of the interview was pretty good.

We went to Appleton Lutz Park, a 3-acre park on the Fox River, in the evening—the long days meant we had so much more time on our hands. We were still getting used to 5 p.m. brightness at 9 in the night. It was a 15-minute drive and at the end of it, we were treated to a spectacular sight of a fabulous scenic place. It has many things going for it—lovely views, a wooden walking pier leading out to the middle of the river, swirling waters, ducks swimming on the lake ... I fell in love with the place, until my shoes went squish on something soft. It was geese poop. The precise identification happened much later, but poo was the last thing I had expected on such immaculately maintained lawns. I'd have pooh-poohed the idea if I hadn't seen it with mine own eyes or stepped on it with mine own feet.

I thought litter was taboo in the U.S., but maybe geese poo didn't qualify as litter. I walked on my toes like a ballet dancer until we reached the comparative safety of the wooden bridge. We strolled along but stopped short when we spotted dead fish in the water. A piscine murder mystery? It stirred the morbid in us, and the 'Spot the Dead Fish' game began. We spotted quite a few, some even on the shore. The topic became an obsession with VK.

The current was quite swift, which seemed a little surprising until Amar gave a laconic explanation—melting snow. The trees still sported the winter look, looking wan and helpless in their leafless state. The grass too didn't appear very green; in fact, it was just beginning to grow in Lutz Park. But the tranquillity of the place was just amazing and we were loath to leave.

By then, the sun had finally set. Amar drove us around Neenah after that. You have to admit that not having people on the sidewalks and having drivers who obey all the traffic rules make for pleasurable drives, especially for the driver. Most heart attacks in India must be triggered by stressful driving experiences. We enjoyed the neat, dimly lit roads, clean air (though our windows were up) and silhouettes of attractive houses. The vast expanse of open night sky made me realise why Americans are such suckers for stories of UFO landings. The sky was crying out for more such stories. We stopped at a garage store before we reached home for some bread, lip balm and some pink tummy upset pills that Amar recommended with such conviction, I felt they must be part of his regular diet.

Dinner for Amar was the spicy chicken biryani that VK had surrendered to the box on the first day—oh, yes, we were stretching the boxes to tatters. VK and I, reverentially disposed towards our delicate stomachs, opted for plain toast.

The apartment was very warm and cosy, all thanks to the heater. I didn't even wear a sweater. After dinner Amar confessed that he had taken us on that long night drive so we wouldn't get jet lagged. 'I loved the ride, but you need not have bothe ...' I fell asleep.

# Fond du Lac

THE NEXT DAY WAS SPECIAL. Arpitha, the raison d'etre we were in the U.S., was arriving from Syracuse. 'By 2.30,' Amar told us. He could barely conceal his excitement, as he left for work early. 'I'll pick her up from the airport.'

I fixed a breakfast of bread and eggs with some coffee. Standard breakfast this was turning out to be. The only mind-blowing decisions I had to make were whether to have the eggs boiled or scrambled or go for an omelette. Two eggs each or one? What stressed me out further was if I should go for plain butter or peanut butter. How about toasted bread? Should I halve the sandwiches and 'triangularise' them, for aesthetic effect? Should I make Bombay toast in Neenah?

My tummy was still not up to the mark and I couldn't quite put my finger on it; I had had only the harmless bread and scrambled eggs today. With another lawn mower, this time manually operated, humming rhythmically in the background, VK and I settled down to read until lunch time. A tomato sandwich topped with pink pill for me, I told myself, while VK went for a jam and jelly sandwich. He seemed not to have learnt his lesson from the octopus; he was now going for jelly.

Arpitha arrived. Exclamations of joy, gurgling laughter and excited exchange of news followed, after which we quietened down to watch a couple of movies while she napped. We had fallen out of the habit of watching movies and it felt like a totally new experience. Both movies, *The Imitation Game*, based on the mathematician, Alan Turing, and the Julia Roberts thriller *Secret of the Eyes*, were absorbing, though I kept taking unscheduled bathroom breaks. Was tomato also a no-no for me? The pink pill hadn't begun working its magic yet.

The day, as it turned out, was for movies. Amar wanted us to get a taste of the cinema theatre experience in the U.S. and took us, that evening, to see the newly released horror movie, *A Quiet Place*, playing at one of the many theatres that comprised Marcus Hollywood Cinema outside Neenah. There were very few in the audience, the screen was huge, the seats were plush, and from the comfort of the chairs, every character on screen, human and monster, looked gigantic—the U.S. emphasis on size is all-encompassing.

The movie revolves around the premise that no sound makes sound sense. Make even the slightest noise and you go kaput. Monsters that are hyper sensitive to sound will jump out of nowhere and kill you. So, we froze in our seats and watched the Abbott family, the only family left behind in post-apocalyptic New York—the rest of the world can eat cake—speak in sign language. Easy, for the daughter is hearing impaired. The family is pitted against the thin, badly put-together aliens with an appreciable dislike for noise. If only a little of that rubbed off on our country.

Sudden noises made us jump, the silences freaked us

out, a nail protruding from a wooden step made us shiver in anticipation ... the experience was nerve-wracking.

Shrugging the monster off, and getting our eyes adjusted to people who were the size of people, we went to a supermarket, Woodman's, on the way back. This one was more gigantic than the Walmart store we had visited, if that were possible.

It was raining when we left Woodman's and it rained all the way home. In fact, rain was our constant companion during the days we spent abroad. It was almost as if we had brought the Kerala rain with us. Except for the occasional respite, it stuck loyally around till we returned.

*ʃ*

It's very difficult to resist the simple allure of rural Neenah, a small Midwest town. Coming from India, where bustling crowds, unmanageable traffic, polluted air and blaring loud speakers can dampen your enjoyment of any outing, I found the quiet tranquillity of Neenah, its abundant natural beauty and bracing air attractive and soothing to the senses. I'd have been happy to spend the rest of my visit going for long walks in the neighbourhood.

But Amar hadn't invited us to the U.S. just to have me go mooning around a 3-mile radius of his apartment. He and Arpitha were determined to give us the time of our lives and with so many wonderful places waiting to be visited and so few days, they had to make judicious choices. Amar was well aware of our love for literature, the great outdoors, places of rugged natural beauty and water bodies, and knowing only too well VK's weakness for museums, which Amar shared, A&A came up with a carefully selected itinerary.

In the ten days we had in Neenah before we left for Syracuse, we managed visits to Appleton, Fond du Lac and Green Bay, cities close to Neenah, and went on enriching trips to Madison, Milwaukee and Door County. We visited lakes, beaches, libraries, unique museums, prominent buildings and botanical gardens, trekked in a State Park, walked along rivers ...

Does it sound like we were rushing like crazy from one place to the other, more intent on being there, doing that, than actually enjoying the experience? Not at all. That, to me, was the beauty and the triumph of our trip. Everything was leisurely—we'd plan to leave at 9 a.m. and set out only at 10.30—except when we ran hell for leather to beat the rain or catch a train. Every outing was spaced out, following the simple principle of dropping a building here or a park there; yet we ended up enjoying and absorbing so much. It helped that evenings were unbelievably long.

Though breakfast remained the mandatory eggs, bread and coffee, Arpitha's entry into our lives brought some variety to the lunch. She made rice, dal and a delicious vegetable dish that must have played a role in settling our temperamental stomachs. We visited Fond du Lac the evening after she reached. From that point, Arpitha became our constant companion, resourceful guide, technology wizard, online booking specialist and our 'go to' person when Amar wasn't around.

Lake Winnebago at Fond du Lac was a forty-minute

drive from Neenah. Fond du Lac, a city in Wisconsin, owes its name to its location. 'Fond du Lac' is French for 'bottom of the lake' and since it is obviously not an underwater city, let's accept the more dignified translation—'the farthest end of the lake'. The lake in question is Lake Winnebago, Winnebago being the name the native American tribe living there had been given by its neighbours. It meant 'people of the stinking water', not a very flattering appellation. But the French retained it, having exhausted their inventiveness with 'Fond du Lac'.

Amar parked near the lighthouse, and we walked about Lakeside Park, with its welcoming pathways, bridges and a petting zoo. A petting zoo, they said, but we saw just one representative, a deer, that leapt away before we could take our hands out of our pockets. A covered bridge was a huge attraction, especially when it drizzled. And most importantly, there was no sign or a whiff of geese poo. In fact, there were no geese at all. No geese, no poo; as simple as that.

Fond du Lac Light at Lakeside Park is more than just a lighthouse that helps mariners sail safe. Built at Lakeside Park during the time of the Great Depression, the iconic lighthouse stands as a beacon of hope for the people of the city. By 1965, it had fallen into disrepair—the floors had to be strengthened or changed, the top deck and the railings had to be replaced, but it remained the same lighthouse when it was restored. It reminded me of a story I had heard of a man boasting about a dagger that had been in his family for generations. 'The blade has been replaced many times, and the handle had to be changed too, but it is the same dagger.'

We have gone up higher lighthouses in Kerala—the Anjengo lighthouse in Varkala, that we often visit, is 130 feet high—but the octagonal shape of the Fond du Lac Light with its flagstone foundation base made the 56-foot structure very attractive. We stomped up the spiral wooden staircase to the observation deck to get a hair- and mind-blowing view of the lake and the lush surroundings. If we wanted a better view, there was a huge telescope to look through.

Clattering down, we walked along the lake and saw, just like we had at Lutz, a lot of dead fish. VK's fascination with them came right back. Instead of the standard, 'Hi, how are you?', VK's opening gambit became, 'Hi, could you tell me why there are so many dead fish here?' He asked a man at the lighthouse. The man turned a deadpan face to him. But VK isn't one to give up so easily. He asked a Black man who was fishing in the gurgling waters and the guy drawled, 'Man, I'm new to this place.' VK then found a father and son duo fishing and asked them too—the father, rather. This man shook his head, looking baffled. Later we heard him shout out the question to a policeman in a boat. VK looked pleased; at least he had got people thinking, even if it was about dead fish.

Our longish walk ended when it began to drizzle again. We quickened our pace; our stroll turned into a gallop. I began to sprint when I sighted the car, not realising it was somebody else's. But the others caught up with me before I could be caught trying to break into a strange vehicle, and we reached Amar's without getting too drenched, though getting even a little wet can be very uncomfortable in cold weather.

We drove a long distance to dinner at an Indian restaurant, The India Bhavan, where we met two endearing waiters, Singh and Godwin. Amar privately called them Sing and Dance. The duo appeared very familiar with Amar; clearly, he frequented the place for his favourite dosas. That's what we all had before returning home in pouring rain.

# Madison

ARPITHA BOOKED A CAB TO take us to the Appleton bus station. We were taking the bus to Madison. Amar had left for work after handing over the reins to Arpitha. And Arpitha, the good sport, led us willingly, armed with her intelligence, cell phone and a whole lot of cards dangling from a band on her wrist, like keys that hang at the end of the saree pallu of Bengali women.

The cab driver, Gary, was a very interesting and friendly guy and VK spoke with him all the way to the bus stop. Neenah was such a small place that almost whenever Arpitha tried to summon an Uber, she got Gary. Gary was a local who was polite, gentle, helpful and, apart from a greeting when he picked us up, spoke only when he was spoken to. And he was spoken to a lot by VK. Through frequent conversations, we could piece together parts of his life. Gary had retired and returned to Neenah to be with his aged mother. Uber suited him perfectly; it brought in some money and kept him occupied without tying him down.

Once when he overheard VK and I wondering whether we should take a sweater with us, he told us that though the sun was shining it might be a good idea to take one along.

Always. He repeated a local joke: 'You don't like the weather in Wisconsin? Wait five minutes. It will change.'

After a short Uber ride, we were at the Greyhound station. Arpitha made enquiries, found out when and where our bus would be parked, scouted around for refreshments and located the washroom. We soon got used to this pattern. Arpitha led, we followed, like baa-lambs. But she would always ask us for our preferences and try to get what we wanted. Like front seats on the Greyhound.

It was not the famous aluminium-grey Greyhound, celebrated in movies, books and songs, but a Lamers bus hired by Greyhound. Hopping on, we got ready for our first bus journey in the U.S.

We exchanged extravagant, 'Hi! Nice-to-see-you!'s with the driver. VK wanted a front seat because of the view, from behind a pane of glass that nearly covered the front of the bus. Arpitha and I chose less visually rich seats right behind VK's.

VK's seat placed him within mouth and earshot of the driver, a medium-sized, muscular gentleman who introduced himself as Steve. VK met his match in Steve, who was a very talkative person. The two conversed non-stop through the three hours the bus took to reach Madison.

Steve had spent a lifetime as a travelling sales person, had retired and was now driving for Greyhound because he liked it. He grew trees on the farmstead where he lived. No, he did not have a unionised job and anyway did not bother about the benefits it would bring because he had invested smartly and was not worried about a second retirement.

What about health care, VK asked, and prudently didn't

mention Obamacare. No problem, Steve responded. He was covered. He did not seem to care much for government support. He could look after himself, he declared, with a certain amount of cockiness that sat comfortably on him. VK wasn't wrong in his hunch, for at one point Steve declared, 'I am a conservative.'

VK cleared his doubts about the trees we passed. VK loves trees. He plans to turn our small yard at home into an orchard, a Garden of Eden; and I've spotted snakes in it.

'Mostly maple,' said Steve. 'Red, grey, oak and ashen maple.' He was a fount of knowledge about trees. 'Most American homes used pine for construction. Not the best quality wood, but inexpensive. And with some maintenance and a layer of paint once in a while, it would last decades.'

He grew different types of pine, fir and spruce on his land. But it was oaks he really wanted to grow. 'Not easy,' he said. 'The soil in Wisconsin is not terribly oak-friendly. Special care has to be taken, particularly with the acidity of the soil. But it's worthwhile.' He smiled. 'Oak wood fetches a lot of money.'

Before VK could introduce the dead fish into the conversation, he got sidetracked for we encountered some road restrictions. 'Why is so much of the road under repair?' he asked instead. The road to Madison wasn't as good as the interstate we had taken from Chicago. There were stretches where repair work was going on and only a lane of traffic was permitted.

'Because the hard winter and the extremely low temperatures during deep freezes causes the tarmac to break up, sometimes,' Steve said. Then he laughed and continued,

'Also, this is Wisconsin, road repair is a year-long, life-long affair.' He then hinted at things that an Indian, always wary of the PWD-contractor-politician nexus, could easily relate to.

But even with the road restrictions, what we noticed was tidiness and discipline. The gravel and other aggregates were arranged in neat piles near where the work was taking place. Signs indicated clearly, and early enough, which way we had to take. Not like in India where the surprise element is a constant. You expect a bridge but splash-land in water instead.

The vehicles moved in a steady and orderly fashion. And Steve kept chatting.

I piped in to ask if he had had any hair-raising experiences while driving a bus. 'Ah, yeah,' he chuckled. 'Once my bus slammed into a deer.' Oh, dear. 'Another time, a wheel from an SUV, two cars ahead, got loose, and came bouncing towards me.'

He did not panic, he claimed, though the speed at which he was driving and the speed of the wheel combined to make it faster and more dangerous than a bullet. 'Lucky the wheel slammed into the front bumper and ricocheted off. A foot or so higher, and it'd have hit the glass right in front of me. I'd have been a goner.' He chuckled again, as if he was narrating a particularly humorous story.

At one point he indicated the low cockpit he sat in, the gauges in front, the switches on the console, a video screen he often consulted and the mirrors that fed him information. 'This is my world. I am not aware of my passengers or anything else behind me. My focus is here,' he stated again, nodding at the equipment around him. 'It's easy to drive these big buses now. Electronics, computers and hydraulics have made it easy.'

He negotiated a big turn. 'Watch,' he said to VK. 'The extra set of rear wheels will lift off the surface so I can take a sharper turn. No effort at all from me.' Though we weren't invited, Arpitha and I watched too.

'Look.' He pointed to a video screen as we reached the tight turn. The wheels moved up when Steve touched a small lever. Down it went at another nudge when the turn was complete. All James Bond style.

'I drive regularly to Chicago and Madison, and sometimes stay over in Chicago. Greyhound is very caring. My work schedule suits me. I'd quit if it didn't.' He was one happy driver.

It would be tragic if, in the not-too-distant future, Steve and others like him were made redundant by AI with driverless buses, lorries and cars, guided by remote or machine control taking over the roads. The best we can hope for is that some humans would be required to maintain the necessary software from California or Bangalore.

We got off at the University of Madison, bidding a warm goodbye to Steve. From there we went food hunting. Arpitha took us to a nearby fast-food outlet for sandwiches. Now, if you think buying a sandwich is the easiest task on earth, you have another think coming, for in the U.S. it is not a simple choice, but a multi-layered decision-making process that challenges the highest intelligence.

'You have to choose, Aunty,' said Arpitha, going ahead.

I looked at the menu stuck on the wall and chose.

'I want a meat sandwich.' And that started the elaborate gastronomical inquisition.

'That's perfect.' The woman behind the counter gave a plastic smile. 'What kind of bread? Regular, brown, wheat, multigrain? Toasted or plain?'

'Plain grain,' I stammered, giving the two words I could recall, as nervous as I had been when I faced the PG viva board.

'What kind of cheese do you prefer? Soft, hard, semi-hard, blue, processed?'

'And the filling. What vegetables? Lettuce, tomato, onion, cucumber...?'

I felt dizzy.

'What meat? Some eggs too?'

'And sauce, ma'am? Tomato ketchup, chilly, mayonnaise, white, blond?'

By then I had a headache. 'An aspirin, that's what I want,' I wished to tell her. 'And pink bread with green cheese, cauliflower filling, kangaroo meat and auburn sauce. Let me see you get me that.'

I don't even remember what I finally got, but I was grateful for something edible. It was giant-sized, so I shared it with VK who had been watching me with some amusement and had smartly decided to give the whole exercise a miss.

We headed to Olbrich Botanical Gardens, the stunning realisation of the democratic vision of Michael Olbrich, an enlightened Madison attorney who wanted to bring the grace and beauty of nature into the lives of everyone—'No greater mistake can be made than the belief that taste and aesthetic sense is a monopoly of the merely well-to-do or purely a product of formal schooling,' he said during his speech in 1921, proposing a garden site near Lake Monona. Bravo.

A series of 'wow's escaped our lips. The beauty of the sprawling 16-acre grounds stretched out before us, and we halted in our tracks. For VK had tripped over his shoe laces with a 'Wow! Awo!' He would have stretched out before us too, but Arpitha and I brought him back to base like a recoiling rubber band. The inviting pathways, the colourful gardens, the lush trees beckoned. We didn't know where to gaze, but we did know where to go—Arpitha and I to the reception and VK to a bench to tie his shoelaces.

A friendly woman 'Hi!-ed' us. 'Entrance to the garden is free,' she said. We grinned.

'But not to the Botz Conservatory.' Now it was her turn to grin, pleased she had fooled us. The egalitarian approach to the enjoyment of nature stopped at the entrance to the simulated tropical world inside Botz.

I watched as Arpitha held up her wrist to choose a card for the tickets. The volunteer opened her eyes wide. 'Cool,' she exclaimed. Had this been India, by now the woman would have got details of the wrist band, where it was available, its price and where she could get it at half its price. This woman swallowed her curiosity and turned to greet the next visitor.

'To Botz,' Arpitha announced.

'Aye, aye.' VK had joined us and we picked up some pamphlets and bought a few magnetic souvenirs before following her to the Botz Conservatory.

We got a warm reception. The glass pyramid housed

tropical trees and plants at a temperature that was warm enough for these and the tropical birds to survive, and thrive. It was welcome warmth. We sighed in ecstasy, peeling off our sweaters.

'Yee, a coconut tree,' I screeched. The trees that hardly attracted a second glance from me at home—unless my self-preservation instincts made me look up whenever I stood directly under a heavily laden one—now became the ticket to a nostalgia trip. 'And coconuts. Real ones.'

'A jack tree.' That was VK. 'And actual jack fruit.'

'And pineapple. Look, a pepper vine too.'

Arpitha looked amused at our excitement, until VK's shout, 'A fishtail palm, and colocasia,' roused her interest.

'What are those?' she asked, bit her tongue and braced herself for the lecture that was bound to follow.

At a pool created by the stream that a smallish waterfall gushed into, I noticed a woman tossing a coin into it. A closer look showed that she wasn't the first to display this quirky generosity—there was quite a fortune in coins scattered at the bottom.

'A wishing pool.' I drew Arpitha's attention to it and rescued her from furthering her horticultural education. 'Let's throw a coin in.'

'Yes, let's. But I don't have change.'

'Ha, I do. Cards don't always do the trick. Any particular denomination?'

'One cent should do,' she said. As I fished out three coins, VK stopped me.

'Not for me,' he looked insulted. 'How can you believe in all this?'

'I don't, but whether you believe in it or not, it's supposed to work,' I quipped, adapting the reply attributed to the Nobel laureate Niels Bohr. When the famous physicist was asked by a journalist, who noticed a horseshoe hanging over the door of his house, 'How can you, a man of science, believe in this?' Bohr is said to have responded, 'Whether you believe in it or not, it's supposed to bring luck.'

Arpitha and I threw the coins and she asked me if I made a wish.

'Yes. I wished Amar gets that job.'

Arpitha looked dismayed. 'Oh, Aunty, you shouldn't say that out aloud; it won't come true.'

'Oh.' Now I was dismayed, but recovered quickly. 'Never mind, let's prove that superstition wrong.'

'Maybe you could try re-phrasing it and throw another coin in,' VK laughed. I rephrased my retort. 'Funny, very,' I said and threw him an exasperated glance.

One quick dekko at the birds, the fish, the orchids and what have you at the conservatory and we came out. The change in temperature was striking. We re-established close contact with our sweaters and moved to the innumerable gardens—sunken, rock, rose and the rest that the place boasted. In the sunken garden, I noticed yellow flowers—daffodils, said the label.

'Daffodils! An actual host of golden daffodils, at last.' I was thrilled. I had studied and taught Wordsworth's worthy words about the flower for all they were worth, without ever having seen one.

The rock garden was next, but what chance did a rock garden have when a golden pagoda-like structure beckoned? All that glitters might not be gold, but this one was.

In minutes we were inside that lustrous structure. It was a sala Thai—a typical Thai pavilion that provides shelter to people. There are only four such salas outside Thailand, and we were privileged to be inside one of them. This was a gift of gratitude from the government of Thailand to the University of Madison for having provided education to the maximum number of Thai students in the U.S. The University of Kerala gets gifts of court notices for delay of results.

'This sala had been assembled by Thai workers without the use of a single nail,' VK said, looking alternately into a pamphlet and his phone.

I gazed uncertainly up. 'Really? But how? The ceiling could fall on our heads.' I sounded like a poor man's Chief Vitalstatistix.

'Nonsense, this is as sturdy as sturdy can be. Solid tiles for the roof. And these gold leaves were painstakingly painted on the pillars. Great craftsmanship.' VK was admiring, though he was no fan of gold.

I grinned. 'The authorities ought to know whom to contact for marketing if they wish to sell off the sala.'

A couple who looked Thai but sounded very American approached VK to photograph them and he obliged, looking as pleased as if he had assisted in a runaway marriage.

VK continued to shine as a photographer, for, a little later, while we walked among trees that were in glorious bloom, a beautiful Black girl came to him with a dazzling smile, her hand holding out a small camera. She was beside a gorgeous tree completely covered with white blossoms, no leaves at all. A young White guy, 'smitten' written all over him, was hanging about her. He was too busy clicking mental shots of his beloved from various angles to take her photos.

'Could you take my picture, please?' She handed VK the camera. 'Just get me in the frame and shoot.'

She took her position in front of the tree, with the white flowers making a striking backdrop. As he took the camera from her, VK's eyes twinkled and he remarked gallantly, 'A flower among flowers.'

The startled boyfriend stopped mooning and started staring at the amateur photographer. The girl smiled; the compliment pleased her. Arpitha looked aghast. She said later she wondered if the chap would bash her father-in-law to pulp, and then how would she explain the metamorphosis to Amar?

I watched, heart in mouth, as the chap's right hand went to his bulging jeans pocket. A gun? VK, blissfully ignorant of the emotions of the people around, clicked the pic. 'One more,' he said, 'just in case the main flower was out of focus.'

'That's done it.' I closed my eyes.

'Here, shoot,' I heard a new voice. My eyes flew open. I saw the chap handing VK his phone. 'One of both of us, please.' Phew.

Pushing our eyes back into their sockets after a few more rounds of the bewitching gardens, we came out. Arpitha booked a cab to go to Wisconsin State Capitol. We went there in comparative silence, VK not going beyond asking the driver for his name and nationality. Either he was overwhelmed by the beauty of the gardens or the beauty of the girl he had photographed, or he was plain hungry. American cabbie James's life story remained a secret.

∫

We learnt later that the aerial view of the geometrically precise and meticulously planned State Capitol shows the shape of a saltire or a diagonal cross with the domed white granite structure standing tall in the centre and white buildings making up the four protruding diagonals. Since we were not hovering over the Capitol, we had no idea about the design, and could only gaze at the Capitol's frontage in wonder.

The massive granite dome that topped the central building would catch anyone's eye, just as it captured ours. It was super—topped by a gilded bronze statue of an elegant woman who was perfectly placed to keep an eye on Madison. And well she might, for a state law prevents any other neighbouring building from being taller.

'Someone is carrying a heavy load,' I commented, for her left hand held a globe with an eagle perched on it, while the right arm was stretched out to symbolise the state motto, 'Forward'. No respite for her head either, for she wore a helmet to signify Wisconsin's lead mining industry, on which a badger, the state animal, sat in state. The Golden Lady, wearing the air of a Greek goddess and the letter 'W' for, what else, Wisconsin, on her chest, is aptly named, 'Wisconsin'. I bet the naming committee spent sleepless nights and several months in serious discussions before coming up with that.

'Weighs more than three tons,' VK observed.

'They must have weighed her before yanking her up there,' I nodded wisely.

We now entered the Capitol through one of the intersections. Entry was free. There were arrows and helpful boards telling us where to go, but bar a few closed rooms, marked 'Private', we generally had the run of the place. It was truly admirable. Here was the building housing the state's most important public office, thrown open to the public. No one came breathing down our necks asking for papers or cautioning us. We had to leave the place at 6 p.m.; that was the only condition. What a symbol of trust.

I can't imagine going into the Secretariat in Thiruvananthapuram or visiting the governor's office without frustrating rounds of handing in applications, proving our bonafides, being sent from section to section, table to table, before getting permission to go into a particular section for a set purpose. And, of course, being asked to come another day.

The dignity and exclusiveness of the interior deepened our sense of awe. You have to hand it to the Americans to build and maintain structures impeccably. Forty-three stones from different parts of the world have been used to build this splendid structure, with the interior of the dome, a mural titled 'Resources of Wisconsin', being another class act. And we felt deeply satisfied as we made our way out at 6 p.m. It's true we hadn't seen the Capitol in Washington DC, but ask any Wisconsinite and they'll tell you that we saw the better Capitol.

It was pouring. Amar had said he would drive down

to join us, and since there wasn't really any shelter in a Capitol that had closed, we walked to Starbucks, my broken umbrella protecting us. Yes, VK's prophesy had come true, the fivefold had now become sixfold, with a rib broken. The spoke hung low, catching my hair whenever it pleased. The handle wobbled and the runner behaved true to its name, running down so that the canopy sat like a floppy hat on Arpitha's and my combined heads. By virtue of being a centimetre taller than Arpitha, I was given the privilege of holding it. After VK got a couple of sharp jabs on his head, he said he preferred getting wet to being scalped, and moved out of the 'protected' space.

We took refuge at Starbucks, ordering muffins first—the cheapest item on offer. American hospitality doesn't run to a Starbucks coffeehouse offering drenched tourists shelter without making them shell out a few precious bucks. Munching on a muffin, Arpitha co-ordinated with Amar who had reached, but couldn't park anywhere. Obviously, parking is not just a Third World problem. When he finally found some space, he gave directions and we took off under the same umbrella on a long walk along the streets of Madison until we finally sighted him.

Since the rain was too heavy for us to even consider further sight-seeing, we turned back and returned home. The rain came hammering down—sheets and sheets of water. Coming from the tropics, the land of monsoons, we thought we had seen rain in all its forms. But this was impressive. It was quite a challenge for Amar, driving in a haze, with only blurry headlights of other cars visible. Poor chap. In effect, he performed the duty of a cabbie, driving a hundred miles to Madison from Neenah just to take us back. The only difference was, VK didn't ask him about his life story or the dead fish in Lake Winnebago.

# Door County

'WE ADORE DOOR COUNTY,' Amar and Arpitha enthused, keen that we experience the 'Cape Cod of the Midwest', more than a couple of hours north of Neenah. They spoke of how spectacularly beautiful it was and how they had enjoyed boating, walking and driving around, on earlier visits.

When we drove there the next day, VK and I found they were right in singing duets of praise. If anything, they had understated the charm of the place. Not surprising, since they had been honeymooning there. Door County (pronounced 'du-er' and not 'door') is on the finger-like projection of land jutting out to the extreme north of Wisconsin. Amar did not want to take us to the tip of the peninsula; Door County is on the narrow strip of land with Lake Michigan on the eastern side and Green Bay on the western. We took one road going north and returned driving along the coast-hugging one. It was the loveliest of trips.

One reason, I thought, was that once we moved away from Interstate 41, we took other, smaller roads, not always built on the principle that the purpose of a road is to take as many vehicles as possible, as quickly as possible, from point A to point B, usually in a straight line. The roads in Door County were narrower, curvier and delightfully devoid of uniformity. They looped, curled, climbed, bent, swirled and meandered through the countryside that in the early spring—the time we were there—had cleaner air and bluer skies than anything we had seen in a long, long time. The roads hugged the natural contours of the land in a way the giant highways did not. Now and then we would drive past a picture postcard town or small city. There were few people about and, wonder of wonders, not many cars either.

There weren't many buildings, and even the tallest, not as high as the trees; the exceptions being the lighthouses. The beaches—the locals call the waterfront areas beaches though both Green Bay and Michigan are only lakes—were clean and mostly deserted. But we couldn't see any land on the horizon. Besides, there were waves along the waterside, so we promptly threw into the waters the Indian idea we had imbibed as children that the seaside had a beach just as a lakeside had a shore.

We were headed for Fish Creek. Better to spend the rest of the day there, Amar said, than drive further to Land's End. When we reached Fish Creek, we found there was no boating available that day. It was too early in the season; there was some ice and snow around to prove it. But we didn't really mind. You could stand anywhere and gaze and gaze and just be happy.

A Latino waiter was the only non-white person we spotted in Door County. I observed at the end of the day that it was one of the most beautiful places I had ever been to and that we were the only blots on the horizon. Not politically correct, of course, but my similarly-tuned family laughed.

Would I recommend Door County to Indians travelling to the States? Yes and no. Yes, if you want quiet and beauty, and to sample some fresh air. Indians don't have to be reminded that they will have to use their passports if they want to breathe fresh air. Yes, if the sight of trees, water bodies, flora and clean little winding roads and small, lovely houses fills you with joy. Yes, if you are a sailing aficionado. No, if you are looking for amusement parks, shopping malls, vegetarian restaurants, places of worship or roads where you can attempt to set new speed records. No, if quiet and peace are things you cannot handle. No, if you plan to take a train, because there are no rail lines in Door County.

And, most importantly, a big 'NO', if you have a bladder that needs to be relieved often. For there was a near total absence of public restrooms. The U.S., I later found out, has a Victorian delicacy regarding toilets, turning a blocked nose to this most basic of needs. In the nineteenth century, it did have what were called 'public urinals', in the early twentieth century they turned into 'Comfort' or, as a wag put it, 'Come-fart stations'. But soon they became victims of cost-cutting measures and disappeared.

To make matters worse, if this lack forces someone to relieve themselves in the open, they are rewarded with heavy fines and some states classify such people as sex offenders. How cruel is that! Americans with a strong civic sense are egging Biden on for a 'pee for free' infrastructure plan to make the U.S. a bladder-friendly country.

After much single-minded scouting, we managed to find a public toilet but I was appalled—it was like the ones I'd seen in the villages of Tamil Nadu when I was a child. There was a toilet seat over a huge hole. No flushing possible, just holding your nose and running out, if you haven't fallen into that black hole of the U.S. I was quite shocked to see a bit of the Indian past showing up in this sophisticated country. Arpitha, who had gone in first, warned me not to look into the gateway to hell. I did, and gagged. There were paper napkins around, of course, and a couple of wash basins, but it was traumatic all the same. It took a while for me to recover from that experience.

The sun finally decided that enough was enough and began to set. And what beauty it unleashed. As we drove back, we kept glimpsing between trees the tantalising sight of the setting sun throwing orange flames over the horizon for a very long distance. We gazed, dumbfounded by the beauty of the flaming colours mingling with the fleecy, tinted clouds, the inky blue of the sky and the patterned green of the trees. Amar, of course, concentrated on the winding roads.

# Green Bay

NO PLACE IN AMERICA, it appeared, was too far from a scenic park where people could gather and relax just by walking around or absorbing all the natural beauty. Just half an hour from Amar's home in Neenah was High Cliff State Park. It is situated on limestone cliffs that were once sacred to the native Americans and owed its name to the location.

Some of the burial mounds built by the indigenous people of America still existed and gave rise to the myth that the place was haunted. That would have added some excitement to our trip, but there wasn't even a hazy outline of a ghost there, only some solid statues of native Americans, the most famous being that of Red Bird, the proud native American chief of the Winnebago tribe who, sadly, died in jail in spite of his hope that the White man would kill him rather than humiliate him. Well, there was a statue to remember him by. Maybe his spirit lives on. We never saw any sign of his people, though.

We wandered around the lower levels of High Cliff, the only state-owned recreational park on Lake Winnebago. If something is called High Cliff, it is sacrilege not to make a superlative effort to climb higher and higher. We explored a couple of simple trails but the higher level, while seeming more attractive, also appeared unsurmountable. The rocky face of the cliff threw a stony challenge. The others were preparing to turn back when I noticed a narrow uphill path hewn on it. The overgrowth had hidden it from view.

I started up. My old climbing skills and my walking shoes didn't let me down—I didn't slide to the bottom. Instead, I clambered to a tougher trail and then hailed the others. 'Hey!'

They hadn't even missed me till then. Now they looked around but not up. 'Where is she?' I heard VK's voice.

'Here.' My delighted shout caught their attention and they all followed, including a very impressed VK. We followed this with another ascent—up an observation tower made of wood this time, and were rewarded with a terrific view of the surrounding areas.

After the exhilarating climbs, we returned to the car and headed to Green Bay. So many of the names in and around Neenah reminded one of the lost culture of the native Americans including, of course, the name Neenah. Green Bay, a forty-minute drive from High Cliff, was different. It was first settled by the French and now home to one of the most famous sports teams in the States—The Green Bay Packers of the National Football League. Amar told us the waiting list for season tickets to their games is probably the longest in the world and the lucky ones who possess it hand it down from generation to generation as a precious heirloom.

Like Fond du Lac, Green Bay's origin was French. It used to be called 'La Baye Verte'. French for Green Bay, so christened by the French explorer Jean Nicolet because of the greenish colour of the water. Had he looked up instead, he might have called it 'Le Ciel Bleu'—'Blue Sky'. If only he had come during a storm and seen the churning, muddied waters, we might just have got a novel name.

Apart from Lambeau Field, the home field of the Green Bay Packers, Green Bay has one superb attraction—The National Railroad Museum. Tucked into a quiet corner near the Fox River, it houses a wonderful collection of old trains and all kinds of artefacts and memorabilia from the history of railways in the U.S.

The moment we entered the museum, the two men rushed ahead and disappeared. Trains and planes have this effect on them. I love trains too, but their love is greater than mine. Arpitha and I knew they had to be somewhere inside, but where? VK was oblivious to my calls, while Amar responded but kept his voice down to such a conspiratorial whisper that Arpitha gave up. We decided to explore the museum at our pace and finally found them inside a train.

The place is fascinating. You travel through time, from the early machines that helped the colonisers move westward, to the giant steam locomotives of the early twentieth century to sleek electric trains with luxurious interiors and jet age looks. Outdoors, in big sheds are many of those locomotives and some of the famous carriages. The most famous is the 'Dwight D Eisenhower', a state-of-the-art locomotive that the U.S. general had used during his travels in Europe during World War II. After making history in Europe, here it was at Green Bay, thrilling visitors along with other famous machines and coaches.

There was nothing resembling the TGVs of France or the bullet trains of Japan. You could make out, as you strolled around, that the automobile and the aeroplane had left railroads behind, at least in the U.S.

Nobody minded that we clambered in and out of those historic trains and engines. It was a special feeling getting into trains that have become history. VK and Amar kept forgetting us in their eagerness to pull themselves up the high steps into engines, and sitting in the driver's seats of giant steam locomotives. We had to yell for them to hoist us up too. Some of the engines had wheels so huge they dwarfed all of us.

Like at all the other museums, we could have spent much, much more time there and not got bored. VK, Amar and I couldn't help recalling the rich and wonderful National Rail Museum at Chanakyapuri in New Delhi that we had visited when Amar was eight. And how did we end this exhausting but totally satisfying day? With a fortifying dinner at Olive Café, of course.

# Paper Discovery Centre and Sue

APPLETON HAD A PAPER MUSEUM, The Paper Discovery Centre, and since the more the merrier was the dictum that guided us where museums were concerned, Arpitha took us there. Amar was at work. She booked the cab after lunch and we piled in. How very easy and pleasant these two had made our excursions.

It was Gary again. Each cab ride with Gary revealed more about the man and his life. Every time we entered the cab, he greeted us like long lost friends and while greeting us, would turn down the volume of the radio. Noticing this happen a few times, VK asked him about it, after we had become more familiar with him. 'I'm a conservative,' he said. 'I listen to Fox News and not all passengers are happy with that.' He flashed a happy smile.

꜋

The Paper Discovery Centre, Appleton, has, we learned later, been described as a boring museum. But since we do not take the expectations we take to a rock concert with us when we visit a museum, we had a very good time. What had been a paper mill, the Atlas Mill, owned by Kimberly-Clark, had been turned into a museum and learning centre. We learned a lot about paper making, its history and the technology behind it. We also became more familiar with the history of Wisconsin.

We even made some paper, along with a group of school children, with a guide hand-holding us through the process. We could choose colours, glitter and embellishments to go into the paper and at the end, VK had a greyish blue, subdued and spartan paper; Arpitha who has a talent for painting, had an artistic creation while I added a little of everything available into the mixture and ended up with a sheet that looked like a Matisse masterpiece.

The guide looked startled. 'Interesting combination,' she gave an uncertain smile. 'And colourful. Yes, very eye-catching. Vibrant, actually.' VK made a pretence of hunting for his non-existent dark glasses. Arpitha, the kind soul, was indulgent. 'Beautiful, Aunty,' she said. Of course, she was referring to the paper.

Soon after this adventure, a man accosted us. He was a Kimberly-Clark engineer, an Englishman who had made Wisconsin his home. I mentioned that our son was working for his company. He—the man, not Amar—had just retired and was slated to be the director of the museum. He said he had more Indian blood than people might believe looking at him. Yes, it would take a great deal of imagination to suspect that—he looked Hollywood white.

A great grandfather of his had served in India during the Raj and had returned to England with an Indian woman for a wife. She had spent the rest of her days in the U.K. He did not know any of this till he had had a DNA test done to find out about his ancestry. Puzzled by how much 'Indian blood' showed up in the test, he had done some research and ferreted out these details. He chatted a while about his plans for the museum; we wished him luck and said our goodbyes.

Next door, practically under the same roof, was a restaurant, 'The Atlas Waterfront Café', or, as the handwritten sign on a white board near the entrance announced, 'The Atlas Waterfront Café and Gathering Room'. It appeared to have been picked out of some design or architecture magazine—it was picture perfect. There was a terrace on one side, overlooking the Fox River, with tables and chairs. It provided a splendid view and a most relaxing atmosphere, but was too cold for us. Even a beautiful scene loses some of its appeal when you have to watch it all hunched up and through chattering teeth.

So, we settled for the proper dining room. It was one of those places where you collected your food from a counter and took it to your table, not uncommon in America. The café, we discovered, was run by an old couple. Sue, the lady at the counter, took our orders, helping us find our way through the menu. Every menu card with unfamiliar food items, hints at adventure, and I was grateful for her assistance. She was the most gracious of hosts. She insisted that we sit at our table. The food would be brought to us. 'You are the only patrons here now,' she pointed out.

Larry, her husband, looked like he was made of paper and seemed even older than the paper mill. We never heard him speak at any point, though he was shuffling around most of the time. What a store of stories he must be, I wondered. There must be a Wisconsin-centred history of the U.S. in the twentieth century in him, I felt. But, alas, we did not have the time or space to find out.

In a corner of the room was displayed a huge dictionary, open roughly in the middle. It was 'The Enormous, Corduroy-clad *Century Dictionary*', a board nearby said. It gave details of the tome. It had over 7,500 pages, was printed in 1914 and now belonged to Sue and Larry. As much a part of Appleton, I thought, as the paper mill and the lovely couple running the café, in what had once been the paper mill's dining room.

Sue joined us after we had eaten. She came over to our table to sit and talk for a while. She was curious about us. We told her the main reason for our visit was Arpitha's graduation and she was very happy to know about it. I mentioned that it was my first trip out of India and that we had landed in Chicago less than a fortnight earlier. We wanted to visit as many museums and parks as we could while in the country, I said.

After a while, she asked, 'If you don't mind my asking, how were those gentlemen at the Chicago airport?' Tactful way, I realised, of finding out if the then president's attitudes had seeped into and hardened the officials at immigration at O'Hare. VK took over. 'A gentleman went through our papers, looked at his computer screen, slammed a seal on a sheet and, instead of saying "Welcome to America", which I expected him to say, looked over my shoulder and shouted, "Next, please." We trudged off, looking for the exit.'

Sue's smile faded. She lowered her head into her cupped

hands. She stayed frozen in that position for a while, before lifting her head to say, softly and with genuine warmth, 'On behalf of my country, I apologise.' Now we were embarrassed and assured her there was no need for an apology. 'We have some of these types in Chicago,' she added with some force.

There was a heap of lovely stuff—handbags and knickknacks—arranged on one side of the café. Wishing to change the subject, I asked her what they were. She explained that she and her husband were organising a sale for charity. 'Generous people like you are a big help,' she said and smiled. Before I could scratch my head and wonder when we had been generous, Sue added that all tips left behind went to charity. 'Your tip was generous.' Amar had taught us to tip and tip well.

Later I commented to Arpitha that I wished I could have been a recipient of the charitable venture—one of those bags in particular was very stylish. VK overheard—he has a great knack for hearing all the wrong things—and shook his head in disapproval. 'When will you leave these very Indian traits behind?'

Sue and Larry, we realised, represented an older, more gracious and cultured America—the polite, hard-working, dignified middle class we had all read about. Like the lumber mills and paper factories of Wisconsin, they were all disappearing. And the values they represented were also fading.

In 2019, almost exactly a year after our visit to The Waterfront Café, Sue and Larry had to close their establishment—an Appleton newspaper, available on the internet, reported it. We read this with a sense of loss, as if we were Appletonians. They could not renew their lease and were on the lookout for something else to occupy their time. The café had been open for fifteen years and was popular with a lot of the locals. We were lucky to have visited when we did.

On the white board outside their café was a sign saying 'Love your neighbor.' There was an asterisk over 'neighbor'. Below that line there was a clear definition of 'neighbor'. It said: 'Your black, brown, immigrant, disabled, religiously different, LGBTQ, fully human neighbour', all in capitals.

Let us salute Sue and Larry Bogenschutz. We didn't just have a nice lunch but a taste of a culture that is evaporating. Small, Sue showed us, was tender. And gentle. And most beautiful. Even in America, the mammoth land of mammoth things.

∫

Amar met us at Neenah Public Library and shepherded us into this fascinating place. It is huge, attractive, well maintained and, whether you are a child or an octogenarian, you can get lost there and be content to stay lost. There is something for everyone—children, teens, tweens, adults and senior citizens.

The children's section with its 'reading tent' extends beyond an enviable selection of books to puppets, stuffed animals, puzzles, games and other attractions, while adults have books, magazines, movies and music to listen to, if they wish. They could also just sit somewhere and dream. Or work.

'Anyone can use the library,' Amar said, as he took us around. 'I often come here to do my work. And borrow books by self-scanning them.'

'Can't people just take books away, then?' I asked, incredulous. 'What high levels of trust.'

I thought of our libraries where some members have made an art of making away with books. We have heard of patrons entering the library with trim figures and leaving it barrel-chested or slightly potbellied.

'Well, not really. There will be a beep if an unscanned book leaves the library,' he chuckled.

'Ah, how could I have forgotten? It's the technology they trust.'

We noticed very old people engrossed in games of scrabbles, cards and jigsaws at cosy tables in corners. Some earnest-looking men and women were working on laptops, at tables by windows with a serene view of the waters. This is a place where time could stand still. And this is one place I would love to sneak out of the U.S. and transport to Thiruvananthapuram; let Neenah reverberate with beeps.

Outside the library stood the statue of the incredible Native American and Ho-Chunk Chief, Glory of the Morning, with a few firsts to her credit. She was the first woman chief of Ho-Chunk, one of the first tribes of Wisconsin and the first woman to be mentioned in the written history of Wisconsin. We looked her up and down before going on a long walk up to the lake near Fox River. People were fishing from the bridge, perfectly still, totally focussed on the line and the water, waiting for the slightest tug. Here, we didn't see any dead fish but even if we had, I doubt any of the people around would have even heard VK's question. They were, like all true-blue fishermen, oblivious to everything else.

We walked along the streets of Neenah and spotted the sculpture of Thomas Jefferson seated on a bench, patting the space beside him, as if inviting us to sit there. We took turns to do that; how could we not oblige the prime architect of the Declaration of Independence?

At the Statue of Liberty Corner, we found a 15-feet replica of The Statue of Liberty, a memorial commemorating the hundredth birthday of the original statue. If Lady Wisconsin guards Madison, Lady Liberty does the honours for Neenah. Close by, we also found sculptures of Abraham Lincoln and George Washington, both frozen on stone benches.

We wound up the day with dinner at Sai Ram, another Indian restaurant. Come to think of it, we had been going mostly to Indian restaurants. But this particular visit was very special for here we discovered something that saved us from the trap of huge portions—the kids' portion. The moment I spotted this on the menu card, I perked up.

'Why not ask for that?' I suggested. 'I'm not hungry at all.'

VK also wanted the same, so that's what we got. Not only was it just right for us, there was an added bonus of a toy at the bottom. I got a top and VK got a soft toy. After that it was always kids' portions for us and we didn't have to shop for toys to take home.

# Milwaukee

THE PRESSURES OF PLANNING TOURS for visiting parents who are also semi-Luddites and helpless in a technology-driven country, working at his job and preparing for his interviews all at the same time had understandably made Amar a little absent-minded. The plan was to go to Milwaukee the next day and we reached the Appleton bus station in the Gary-driven Uber to find that Amar had booked tickets once again for Madison.

The chirpy 'hi'-ing woman at the counter pointed this out to Arpitha. As always, I stood by her side, a most ineffectual right-hand person. Arpitha insisted the booking was to Milwaukee. After some back and forth she understood who was responsible for the mix-up. Now the topic shifted to cancelling the tickets and re-booking.

'No cancellation possible, ma'am,' the woman said, her smile fading.

'The bus to Milwaukee is moving,' a young guy, leaving the office after getting his ticket, threw over his right shoulder, heaving his bag over his left. He looked pleased at having been the bringer of glad tidings.

It had the desired reaction. We gave a collective start, and VK took position for the fifty-metre dash.

'You can take the next,' the woman at the counter shrugged. I love the way Americans shrug their shoulders. They speak an entire language using them. 'But no cancellation,' she warned. It took a while for us to sort it out—for Arpitha to sort it out, rather. I just watched. The technological brouhaha was beyond me. If either of the active participants looked at me for confirmation, I'd nod, looking wise and then realise the nod was mistimed—I was actually undoing what Arpitha was trying hard to rectify. So I did the next best thing. I skipped to the loo.

The lady was not for turning, and we didn't really have a leg to stand on. How do you convince someone that you absentmindedly booked tickets to the same place you'd been to a couple of days back, and request a change of tickets to the right place instead?

We ended up buying fresh tickets and once that was done the smile was back, dimples and all. She suggested, rather vaguely, that we could try later for an online reimbursement for the erroneous booking. What she probably wanted to say was, 'Whether you do it now or later or never, whether you get anything at all is none of my concern. Now please get the hell out of here.' No, I'm being uncharitable; she was rather sweet, actually. Anyway, Arpitha acted on her suggestion after we returned that evening. All to no avail. No refund, thank you.

It was an actual Greyhound bus this time. Because of the confusion, by the time we got into the bus, the seats in front were already taken. So VK couldn't get the driver's life history out of him. He couldn't get anything out of the person seated next to him either, for that happened to be me. I could give any self-respecting Trappist monk a run for his money when I'm on a moving bus or car. To keep travel sickness at bay, I become motionless and silent, concentrating with such keenness on the road ahead that it would put a secret service agent to shame.

VK had to settle for his own thoughts and the absorbing scenes we passed all through the hour and a half the bus took to cover the hundred-mile distance. We were very fortunate to have travelled in a Greyhound bus, for, a few months after our visit, Greyhound shut down its bus service to northeast Wisconsin, leaving the roads to Amtrak and Lamers. For Wisconsinites, it was the end of an era.

We managed a quick lunch at the Milwaukee bus station and choking over the strange combo sandwich I seemed to have ordered, we were off to Milwaukee's much lauded natural history museum—the Milwaukee Public Museum. And no wonder, it richly deserved all those plaudits and more. This is a must-see museum and for me, the best among all we had visited so far, and there were quite a few jostling for the top spot.

You succumb to 'A Sense of Wonder' when you climb the wide staircase to the first floor and a magnificent skeleton of a humpback whale, in the company of a huge number of other rare worthies, greets you. Skeletons aren't exactly calculated to inspire rhapsodies. But this one is special. The museum boasts of a mindboggling number of singular artefacts, but its chief attraction lies in its dioramas—exhibits that are full-size or miniature models. From dioramas that depict the geological history of Wisconsin when it started out as a shallow sea to a representation of the streets of old

Milwaukee, from startlingly realistic scenes of life in Asia, Africa, Europe and the Americas to guiding you through the ancient civilisations, from taking you for an awesome glimpse of ocean life to encouraging a stroll through rain forests, it is a jaw-dropping experience.

At the replica of a typical English village, VK realised his childhood dream—to ride on an actual penny farthing. Well, not completely, for he could only sit on it, it being fixed to the ground, but he could pretend to pedal it and that was good enough.

This time we were able to meet Amar without any problem at the rendezvous decided upon—outside the art museum.

'Let's go for a walk,' said Amar who wanted to stretch his long legs. Our legs had been well stretched to thin, spindly appendages by all that walking in the museum, but before Arpitha or I could suggest a short break, VK whipped open the map of Milwaukee and the enthusiastic father-son duo went ahead, the map flapping into their faces, taking byways and turns according to its dictates, bumping into people and apologising instead of saying, 'Hi! Great way to meet you.' We trotted after them to the Historic Third Ward in Downtown Milwaukee to soak up some history.

It was almost like the walk at Dubai airport; we had no idea when it would end. Just when I felt I had enough history in me for two generations, they stopped and waited till we caught up with them. When I approached, Amar announced, 'Let's go back.'

'All the way back?' I panted.

'We have to; the car's parked there.'

How I longed for an autorickshaw that we could flag down by the simple act of stretching a hand, and paying the driver in cash when we reached our destination. My friend Sumi's niece, Ansu, who lives in the U.S., loves the autorickshaw so much, it is the main reason she's enthusiastic about a visit to India. The moment she gets here, she clamours for a ride in the 'Indian car'—her name for the auto. Oh, Americans, you don't know what you're missing. At that moment, I knew pretty well what I was missing.

We took off on the return marathon and reached the finish line at our limping best, tongues hanging out.

'We're going to Bollywood,' Amar said as we crawled into the car.

'Bollywood?' I was in no mood for a movie. 'A restaurant,' he grinned. I groaned, expecting a garishly lit place, loud Hindi songs, dashing waiters and heavily made-up waitresses. But there was nothing glamorous about Bollywood Café, and a good thing too, for after all that time in the museum, only dinosaurs would have interested me. But the chicken was decent.

# Syracuse

THE NEXT LEG OF OUR visit was about to start. Amar had gifted me a new phone a week after we reached—my first smart phone. I had been clinging on to my ancient feature mobile that, like an old family retainer, had served me very well, notwithstanding an occasional malfunction. Smarties might dub this a dumb mobile, but being dumber, I was devoted to it. However, in the U.S., it was useless and I had to give in. Amar had been tutoring me on some phone basics, and on the day we were leaving for Syracuse, he wanted me to use my phone to book an Uber.

'You must,' he insisted when I protested. 'How will you learn otherwise? What would you have done without us?'

'Not come to the U.S. for one,' I grinned.

Anyway, with three pairs of eyes watching every nervous fumble, I managed to book a cab. Gary was the driver again, and we went to Appleton to take an evening flight to Minneapolis, made so familiar to the world because of the George Floyd tragedy. Amar had stayed back and would join us in a couple of days.

We were soon off in a small, uncomfortable Delta regional jet, crouched on our seats. If my short legs were cramped for space, I wondered how my son, at six feet, of which four feet are legs, managed short flights. He probably emulates my fivefold umbrella.

When the plane landed, I found my right ear blocked and going pop, crackle, pop in spite of the ear plugs. I found Arpitha looking distressed; her right ear was blocked too, and for her this was the first time. Experienced me decided to guide her out of it. 'Swallow, à la Captain Haddock,' I suggested.

'Swallow? Swallow what? How? There's nothing to swallow. What's the captain's name again? I can't hear, Aunty. Is he our pilot?'

'Forget the captain.' I raised my voice. 'Pretend to swallow. Use your ear muscles to unblock the ear.'

'Can't. Do ears have muscles?'

'Two,' I said. I'd asked this at a quiz I had conducted. 'Vestigial.'

'West of what, Aunty?'

'Never mind. Shake your ear lobes.'

'Aunty, it's got unblocked. With a pop.'

So had mine, and I realised I had stumbled upon a new way to clear a blocked ear—just talk at cross purposes.

From Minneapolis we took a flight to Syracuse. This plane was bigger and we were actually given something to eat, even if it was only a miserable, micro-mini chocolate biscuit. We went to the baggage area and my eyes popped out when I saw Deepa Ram, our host at Syracuse, waiting there. Was I seeing things? In India, no one is allowed anywhere inside the airport, but not so in the U.S., I learnt. It was her all right; I could see her steadily and she was whole. It was so good to spot her there.

I had taught Deepa Ram for her BA and MA. Not only did she survive my classes, she wanted me to stay with her at Syracuse. We had re-established contact when she got in touch to ask for an autograph for her daughter, Nandika. She said that Nandika was such a huge fan of my *Butterfingers'* books, she had actually told her school librarian to replace all the Roald Dahl books with the *Butterfingers* series. That made me her instant fan. Sorry, Roald.

We met Deepa's husband, Ram, and soon reached her spacious and beautifully kept apartment. It was late and Nandika, tired of waiting up, had gone to bed. She had left a note of welcome on the table, and all her *Butterfingers* books in a basket with another note—this one of warning—tucked in: 'Too precious! Don't touch. Because I love them. Mine!' The best warning I've ever received. After dinner, Ram dropped Arpitha at her lodging.

Deepa spoilt us silly with delicious south Indian food interspersed with visits to the Liverpool library and Onondaga Lake the next day. We saw a lot of people walking their dogs and Nandika went around petting some of them. I noticed that if any dog pooped, the owner used thin gloves to scoop it up with devotion and care, reversed the gloves and dropped the booty into a waste bin. If only the geese at Fond du Lac and dogs who are walked outside my gate in Thiruvananthapuram also had owners who followed them around to do the honours.

What happened at the Onondaga Lake turned me into an admirer of the U.S. weather forecasters. It was a bright afternoon, blue skies, gentle breeze, great views and the rest of the trappings. We were enjoying a walk when Deepa's phone beeped. 'It'll rain in ten minutes. I got an alert,' she announced.

'Ha, you've got to be joking,' I said. 'Look at how clear the sky is. Surely even the U.S. needs the help of rain clouds for rain?'

'I don't know, but such alerts are generally correct.'

'Then they got it wrong this time. There must always be a first time. Let's walk further.'

After we had walked a good distance, I turned to Deepa. 'Where's your rain?' I lifted my face to the sky and plop! A drop of water fell into my eye. Bombed by a bird. That was my first thought but there was no feathered friend in sight; instead, I saw a few unfriendly-looking clouds. From where had they come?

As if it were a stage scene obeying the director's cue, the clouds changed colour and joined forces to form one big shapeless mass. Lights! A forked lightning flashed in the distance. Music! An obedient clap of thunder. Action! And we took to our heels as rain came pouring down with strong gusts of wind malevolently blowing against us, slowing us down. It was exactly ten minutes since Deepa got the alert. We reached the car soaking wet. Once we were home, dry and sipping cups of hot tea, Nandika giggled. What a story to tell her friends.

With Arpitha not around, Deepa took over and booked a cab to Syracuse University the next morning. It was 8 and early by our standards. As Deepa and I settled in at the back, VK got ready for a cosy chat with the driver. 'Are we your first customers of the day?'

'Naw,' the cabbie drawled. 'Been driving since three in the morning.'

'Three?' VK exclaimed. 'How come?'

And we listened to another story.

This gentleman had retired after more than three decades as a 911 responder. As a cab driver, he did twelve-hour shifts, starting at three in the morning.

VK sat up, all ears. A 911 responder? He plied him with a volley of eager questions.

'What kind of calls did you get? How did you respond? How was it like, back in the analogue days, coping with the demands made on you? Was it stressful?'

The cabbie didn't seem to mind. 'In the beginning, we used printed maps. Even as I ask a caller for their full address, one hand would be pulling out the correct folder from a collection near me. You had to be very quick, very alert. By the time I got the details of what the problem was, I already had the exact location identified on my map.'

'Wow.' I couldn't help interrupting. 'And all without the aid of computers.'

He half turned to smile. 'Yes. And when computers came along, they transformed the job but increased the work load. When I began, Syracuse was a small university town and the emergency centre only responded to calls from within it. Now with computers to help, a huge swath of New York State has to be handled by the operators.'

'That's the same problem everywhere,' VK said, and Deepa and I nodded. Don't we know how computers have helped employers tighten the electronic noose around the necks of their employees and kept them on call 24/7?

He was a contented retiree and was driving to make a little extra money and to keep himself occupied. We passed rows of near identical wooden houses lining the streets of Syracuse.

'Look at the houses,' VK observed.

'All clones,' I nodded.

'Most of those were put up in the post-World War boom,' the driver explained. 'Now they are in bad shape because landlords let them out to students who rarely stay beyond two years and the landlords never bother to keep them in good repair.'

By then we had reached Arpitha's house and learnt first-hand exactly what he had meant. Waving the friendly man goodbye, we entered the house rented by Arpitha and some other students and felt we had entered another world, a strange, spooky world. It was a 121-year-old wooden house that used to be a motel. Now it had been converted by the assiduous indifference of generations of students into a ramshackle, tumbledown building. All over the world, landlords hesitate to rent their apartments to students for precisely this reason.

'How do you stay here?' I asked Arpitha who welcomed us in. Paint was peeling off the walls and spiders lurked in dark corners. I looked around a little anxiously as if I expected ghosts to shimmy out of cracks and say 'Boo!' I jerked my head up, eyes to the ceiling, half expecting leering bats to be hanging upside down.

Arpitha saw this and laughed. 'Aunty, most houses here are like this. Ours is a better one. In the beginning we were quite scared, but we soon got used to it.'

At this point, the wooden floorboards creaked under our feet. I jumped. Deepa merely looked startled and exclaimed, 'What's that?'

It turned out to be no spirit, but a rather solid VK, walking up and down, testing the wooden floor which groaned, creaked and squeaked in protest with every step he took.

Arpitha gurgled. 'This is nothing. I'll take you to the basement. We have our washing machine there.'

She led us to the rickety wooden staircase and we tiptoed down, holding hands, quite certain a step would give way any time. If we stumbled, we'd tumble down together. We finally reached the bottom intact and stared at the eerie, musty basement which made the floor above seem like the last word in sophistication. The cobwebs festooning it would have made Miss Havisham burst into song. There was graffiti on the walls and thick dust everywhere—on the floor, on some abandoned pieces of art, scattered knickknacks and broken furniture, not to mention clouds of it that we had kicked up. A washing machine stood in a corner, looking like it could do with a wash. VK began to sneeze, the signal for all of us to pirouette to the stairs and race back to civilisation, pulling cobwebs off our faces. Was it student accommodation or a lesson in American history?

After that unnerving experience, Arpitha took us around the neighbourhood. We met a couple of her housemates, and I secretly tipped my non-existent hat to all of them for living in that ghostly dwelling and actually completing their courses without becoming batty. Maybe they didn't do much washing. After all, in a cold place, what would it matter? Ask Queen Elizabeth I whose bath day was rumoured to coincide with her birthday.

We reached Syracuse University and got our first glimpse

of a prestigious U.S. university—huge, impressive buildings, sprawling campus, immaculate lawns with sculptures scattered about, welcoming pathways, an art museum, theatres and magnificent libraries with an admirable selection of books even in the Humanities section, though Syracuse was primarily a tech university. A memorial wall dedicated to the thirty-five students killed in the horrific Pan Am Flight 103 air crash over Lockerbie, Scotland, in 1988, tugged at our heart strings. Arpitha took us to her department where we walked along the corridors and peeped into lecture halls.

Amar, who had reached Syracuse, chose to remain in the ghost house to prepare for his next interview—the Bath part of it, probably—and Arpitha went back to join him. We had lunch at a local joint before returning to Deepa's.

Nandika was beside herself with excitement when we returned; she had been waiting impatiently to tell us that her entry at the science fair in her school had won a prize. We were thrilled and VK took her, next morning, to Barnes and Noble to buy her books as a reward. We ended the day by keeping our destiny with Destiny USA, the largest shopping mall in New York where Deepa and Nandika went on a scary virtual space ride. Just watching their faces gave me vicarious fright. They came out of it, slightly disoriented and unsteady on their feet, but dinner soon set them right.

The big day arrived—Arpitha's graduation day. The programme was scheduled for 3 p.m. and Ram dropped us at Arpitha's residence well before that. We entered the house, laden with flowers, looking and smelling like rose bushes, to find that Arpitha had already left. We were hoping to download the bouquets on her, but would have to haul them to the university. As soon as Amar was ready, he called a cab that took us to the venue.

The solemn function began at exactly 3. Entering the hall from the back, the dignitaries led the ceremonious procession along the aisle to take up their places on stage. The graduating students followed and immediately there was a ripple of excitement. All of us in the hall craned our necks to spot our special person. After my neck developed a solid crick, Amar identified her, naturally. Arpitha, looking every bit the studious scholar in her gown and cap, walked majestically forward, but her eyes were darting around, looking for us. When she came close, we hailed her in a loud whisper. The moment she saw us, she flung something that Amar caught before it hit his head. Great catch.

'What's that?' I was intrigued. 'Not part of the graduation ceremony, is it?' I knew graduates threw their caps in the air after the function, but I hadn't heard of them throwing things at their families during the march.

'House keys,' Amar giggled, pocketing the bunch, and took off to the front to take better pictures. The speeches were very good, crisp, occasionally witty and never exceeded the time allotted for each. The degrees were awarded, and when Arpitha's name was announced twice, since she was in two sets of subjects, the loudest applause came from our corner. By 4.30 the formal function was over and it was celebration time.

The inevitable outdoor photo sessions followed. The sky had been overcast the whole day, making the weather very chilly. Fortunately, the rain limited itself to threats. The students tossed up their caps—a gesture that has become a mandatory part of any graduation ceremony—and then the girls threw off their graduation gowns to reveal the stylish outfits they wore under them.

Looking at their beaming faces and happy poses in the photos they must have posted immediately on social media, who would have guessed they'd have been shivering in those off shoulder, short dresses? They deserved special Oscars for acting brave. I was feeling very cold too, in spite of being adequately covered in my saree and sweater, but the males appeared very comfortable. Men always have an advantage at formal functions for their suits are designed for warmth, while a woman's glamour quotient is directly proportional to the skin exposed. Why formal functions, just think of all those song sequences in Indian films where the hero rolls down snow-capped hills, well protected in a sweater, muffler and cap, while the poor, skimpily clad heroine responds with a happy song from lips that tremble with cold masquerading as passion.

Realising it was getting late for we were taking the train to Niagara, we rushed to Arpitha's house, leaped out of our formal clothes, pulled on our casuals—my dependence on jeans was near total—heaved the bags up, dived into another cab and sped to the station. This was our first visit to a railway station in the U.S. But first things first—Arpitha smelt out a Subway outlet there and bought us something to appease the gnawing hunger pangs. There's nothing like food, even that composed of mostly unidentifiable components, to raise your spirits, and, munching on the peculiar-tasting sandwiches, we were soon in the right mood for the next adventure.

# Niagara

WE WERE TAKING THE Amtrak Empire Service, if you please, making us feel regal. We promptly fell in love with Amtrak the moment we started our journey from Syracuse to Niagara. It looked and felt like a toy train compared to the anaconda style long-distance trains we were used to in India.

We were met by a conductor who greeted us with typical American cheer, pointed out our seats, tucked our ticket stubs into the seatback and moved on. These seats were roomier and, unlike in most Indian trains, largely empty. So, if something on the other side attracted your attention, you could hop over to another window seat across the aisle. But the pace, unpredictability and lack of punctuality made us feel at home. And, for perhaps the first time on our trip, we went through places that did not look freshly manicured and polished.

Quite often I was reminded of some of the scenes that flit past during train journeys in Kerala—the hewn cliff sides, the trees, the greenery, the water bodies. And we were especially reminded of India when the train stopped in the middle of nowhere for a long time and for no apparent reason. The difference was that here one didn't jump out to investigate. In India a lot of people would have been out by now, walking up and down, trying to find the reason for the halt and adding their own speculations to what they were told. Have Americans been conditioned to be uncurious or is it because of practical reasons, for once the doors are closed, they cannot be opened except by someone at the controls? I would like to believe it is the latter.

✕

Aha, the Kodak sign! That had to be Rochester. And it was Kodak town. We gazed and gazed and were so absorbed in drinking it in, we forgot to photograph it. How ironic. Soon the train braked at Rochester. In fact, it had only two official stops—Rochester and Buffalo—from Syracuse to Niagara.

By the time Arpitha and I decided to track down the buffet car, and like all good mysteries found it at the end, it had closed. The woman in charge was supremely indifferent to our request for a bite to eat. Our hungry faces, our longing glances at all the food that was spread out, cut no ice with her. We pleaded, but we might as well have been addressing a stone wall.

That's the problem with the U.S. They are such sticklers for rules they will not make an exception even during exceptional circumstances—like when a couple of starving Indians appeal for food with tears of hunger in their eyes. She uttered mechanically, 'Sorry, we are closed.'

I wanted to tell her, 'What are you talking about? Look

at these big fat rolls lying open before us.' Yes, bread rolls in small heaps were enticingly lined up on a counter. This would never have happened in India. First of all, nobody particularly adheres to a closing time. The closing time is when everything gets sold. And on the off chance there indeed is a closing time, hungry women would not be sent away empty-handed or empty-mouthed.

We got some water, though—thank goodness for small mercies—and we retuned, gulping down the elixir of life. As we walked back, I asked Arpitha what they'd do with all that food.

'Trash it,' she said matter-of-factly.

'What? All that fresh food just thrown away?' I couldn't believe it.

'Yes,' she said and narrated her experience of working at the canteen in Syracuse University. She had been appalled in the beginning at the huge quantities of food thrown away every day but soon understood nothing could be done about it—it was just how things were.

It was late in the night when the practically empty train reached the Niagara Falls station.

Our train was delayed, we were hungry, a little tired and it was very, very cold. The platform was empty and gave out sinister vibes. The comfort of crowds and well-lit places is starkly apparent at such times. As we made our way to the exit, we noticed three or four people standing in a group at the doorway to the station. They turned out to be the crew of the train, waiting to wish us good night and apologise for the delay. Lovely gesture; I don't think we'd see this in India. Besides it wouldn't be practical. Apart from us, there were only two other passengers. A trainload in India always meant hundreds of people. Here it was six—four foreigners and two natives. Not counting the Amtrak employees.

Amar booked a cab and till it reached, we kept looking over our shoulders, behind and around us, as if some gun-toting, trigger-happy villains would show up. When we dragged ourselves into the motel Amar had booked, it was 11 p.m. The motel was run by a Gujarati. It may be stereotypical to say this, but Gujaratis have traditionally been famous for their shrewd business sense and we weren't surprised to find one of them running the show here. There was a lone guy at the check-in counter, looking a little impatient. He hastened through the formalities, handed us the key, switched off the lights, locked up and disappeared forever.

We went to the room and set our bags down. It was huge, with two large beds, and looked comfortable, except that it was quite cold. We thought the owner, with parsimony coursing through his veins, would have turned the heater off till we arrived, and would have turned it on now. It'll soon be warm, we consoled ourselves.

'Let's go to the Falls,' Amar suggested. He had found out that we might just catch the illumination. 'Shouldn't miss the opportunity. They might turn off the lights soon.'

Arpitha said she'd like to stay back and sleep off her tiredness; she had had an exhausting day. VK and I trotted out **after Amar** obediently. We booked another cab and reached **Niagara** to be greeted with an absolutely fabulous sight.

Niagara Falls has followed me from my childhood with

its attractive presence in my social studies textbook, in articles, in picture postcards and the 'believe it or not' descriptions of daredevils going over it in barrels, but nothing really prepared me for the actual sight. The swirling waters rushing to cascade over with a roar, the sense of its might, the beauty of the artistically lit up falls made me speechless. The weather also contributed to my speechlessness; my teeth did all the chattering when we walked around, viewing the falls and the changing colours from various angles. But soon the chilly conditions couldn't be ignored. Though I was wearing a sweater and a warm puffer jacket, my hands were getting stiff with the cold.

'Where are the gloves I got you?' Amar asked.

'In ... my ... bag,' I stuttered, feeling foolish. This was a repeat of what had happened at Chicago airport. Instead of getting exasperated, Amar gave me his gloves. He said he didn't mind the cold much, being used to it after his stints in Boston and Wisconsin.

I felt very bad, and offered him one glove, but he laughed and just thrust his hands deep into his pockets. 'This works,' he said. VK quietly followed suit. He too had forgotten the gloves. Hands warmed and mind eager to prolong the fantastic experience, I dragged both of them on an additional round of the illuminated glory.

Amar booked another cab to take us back. What a convenience, these Uber cabs—they are around any time of the day or night. Since I'm not an Uber booking person and hopeless with apps, this peering into the phone, guiding your thumbs all over it, and then have a cab appear out of nowhere is nothing short of a miracle—straight out of *The*

*Arabian Nights*, except we fly on solid ground, not magic carpets.

We returned to a stone-cold room well past midnight. Arpitha appeared to be fast asleep and after a quick skip to the loo, brushing of teeth and change of clothes, I dived like a porpoise under the cold blankets hoping the warmth from my body would make the bed warmer, though, if you ask me, I felt there was only freezing blood wending through my veins. VK went to the restroom after me. Chivalrous behaviour is so cool.

I had just drifted off to sleep when at about 2 a.m. VK woke me up saying the bathroom door wouldn't open. He had his torch (the one recommended by Robin Jeffrey, though Robin might never have had this particular use in mind) in one hand and was twisting and tugging at the knob with the other. Next, he kicked the door, used brute force, or whatever his 58 kg weight could provide, and, for good measure, muttered some choice words, but the door was impervious to any form of attack.

Declining my offer of help, to my guilty relief, for the bed was becoming snug, he stepped out to look around the motel compound for a restroom. The motel's office was closed, and nothing happened when he rang a bell placed next to a handwritten sign that said 'Back at 10 a.m.' He stormed back and woke up Amar who was in deep sleep. Amar knocked into a bed and a table before stumbling to the bathroom door. But his efforts were also in vain. The door seemed to be locked from the inside.

Now both went to the front office and returned, unsuccessful. I heard Amar ask his father, 'Can you hold it in till the morning?' Prompt came the reply, 'No.' I bet Amar gave a silent sigh. 'Oh, parents.'

He sought the help of that one instrument wonder, the smart phone, located an all-night diner and booked an Uber to take them there.

Since I wasn't with them during their nocturnal adventure, I thought it best that VK himself recount it to readers. Here is what he said, in VK's voice, untampered.

'The Uber dropped us at the local Denny's, a chain everyone seemed to know about. I walked in and was surprised to find a well-lit, crowded, noisy place. So many people eating at 3 in the morning!

'We were led to a table near one that had a group of youngsters with haircuts, jewellery, tattoos and clothes that suggested that much attention had been bestowed on each. They were in the middle of a meal and a conversation. The moment our order was placed, I headed to the washroom—the reason why we were there in the first place.

'I returned to the sound of raised voices. Unusually for America, the whole restaurant could hear every word each one of them was saying. The group was split evenly into the two main racial groups in the northern parts of the U.S. Soon an argument broke out. Everyone contributed, but the leaders were a Black guy and a White girl, sitting next to each other. Each referred to the other with a word normally used for female canines but was an obscenity when hurled at human beings. All this was, however, in good spirits. The topic of dispute was whether an iPhone was better than a regular phone that used the Android operating system. A lot of four-letter words were flying around but it was actually just a technological evaluation.

'We were waiting for our food when the argument began. Amar smiled gently at me, indicating that it was all fine and we should carry on. When an old lady, one of the two waitresses at the place, came to enquire about anything else we might need, she bent low over our table and said softly, "I am sorry, guys." Amar quickly assured her that we were all right. We really had no objection to the natives speaking in their mother tongue. I even thought of thanking her for placing us in what appeared to be the middle of a scene out of something like *Pulp Fiction*, albeit a less witty one.

'As we rose to leave, one 'b' was telling the other which orifice of her body she should shove her phone into and what she should proceed to do with it after that initial move had been accomplished; all to widespread applause and laughter from the others at the table.

'We were at the counter, settling our bill, when the cashier, an elderly White gentleman, bent forward and whispered, "I am sorry, guys." No problem, we said. The food and service were good and we were satisfied.

'We walked out into the night, much edified. I even thought it was a good thing the door was jammed. This—a slice of authentic American life—

was not something on a normal tourist's menu, and I thought of it as a bonus.

'Another Uber ride and we were under our blankets at the motel. But the night had not quite ended. Blame it on the cold weather, but I woke up again a little after 5 and the knob of the bathroom still would not open.

'But I could not wait. It was light outside. I prowled around looking for some place where I could do what Swachh Bharat did not want me to do. There were cars on the road, but no one to whom I could have turned to for help. Close by, between the walls of two buildings, I noticed a vacant plot. It was fenced and had a small metal gate which opened at a push. Inside was a sight I had not yet seen in the States. Uncut grass, a few small trees, some used automobile tyres and so on. I glanced up the walls. No windows were open but I looked carefully around for video cameras.

'A vision passed through my head. I was standing in front of a magistrate, having been caught on camera doing this very un-American thing of peeing outdoors. The judge was stern. He looked at the evidence and then gave me a lecture on how I had sullied the pristine surface of his land and should be given exemplary punishment. "Six months!" he growled and brought his gavel down.

'Even this vision did not reduce my urge. Making sure I was unobserved by human eyes and hoping that there were no hidden cameras, I went behind a tree and made my life less miserable and returned.'

Meanwhile, I was drifting in and out of sleep, worried that we might be held responsible for ruining the lock of a restroom and may have to pay a fortune in damages. When you are in an alien country, all sorts of fears can assail you. I also kept thinking of the immediate problem before us, and the probable solutions if the door continued to remain stubbornly closed. If only VK had been a bomber pilot, he'd have had a piddle pack—a bag that had absorbent beads in it—handy for an emergency. But college professors being equipped with only sling bags that would be woefully inadequate for the purpose, we had to look for other practical options. Maybe we could use the empty water bottles. Or ziplock bags. Or ... My imagination would have tripped along thus when I heard the two men return. Happy they had come back and relieved they had relieved themselves, I slept off.

I awoke early next morning to a lot of noise around. Arpitha had woken up and had just come to know what had transpired the night before. Quite indignant about it and about the tomb-like cold in the room, she had marched to the office, Amar in tow, and a little later, two things happened at the same time. The room began to get warmer and a man walked in with some tools in his hand, followed by A&A. Wordlessly, he stuck a long screw driver into the lock of the door, twisted it about, and hey presto, the door opened.

He went off, as silently as he had entered, and left us looking at one another, baffled. One thing was clear: this wasn't the first time. We found marks on the door jamb probably made by the same screw driver when other guests had been locked in or out. I felt glad; at least we wouldn't be sued for ruining property, a quite likely outcome in a land where suing is as normal as breathing and insurance is your oxygen cylinder.

The moment VK found the door open, he shot in like a rabbit that had spied a carrot. Well, really. Arpitha then told me what had happened. She had spotted another number near the door on which VK had found the 'Back at 10 a.m.' legend. It was a number for use in case of an emergency, which VK hadn't spotted without his glasses. Probably when Amar accompanied him the second time, he had allowed his father to do the reading and hadn't double checked. But Arpitha was nothing if not thorough.

She had called up that number and had spoken to the owner's son. I don't know what she told him, but he had turned up immediately—with the screw driver. Probably he slept with it by his bedside. She also narrated how she had got him to turn up the heater. He had tried to tell her the heater had been on the whole night, and she had retorted, 'In your room, maybe, not ours.' And when a woman turns on the heat, the man will turn on the heater.

We flopped back on our beds in the now warm room, but not for long. Niagara and a return journey lay ahead.

At 10, we got ready and VK, Arpitha and I went to the Falls. This time, Amar stayed behind; he was very tired and had to check out at the right time too. He said he'd meet us at the railway station. Arpitha warned us, as our cab approached the Falls, that there would be long queues for the Maid of the Mist boat ride. Niagara is one of the most touristy places in the U.S. and for the first time we got that quintessential touristy experience. Though it wasn't as bad as we had feared, it was very crowded. We saw a few familiar faces from the graduation day and any number of Indians. I heard VK speak in Malayalam to some people; it's good he didn't know Telugu. Else he'd have been speaking to half the people there. Our friend Nizar, in San Jose, had tried to dissuade us from going to Niagara. He said we might as well go to Hyderabad.

We were given blue raincoats as soon as we stepped on the boat. These were pre-Covid times; and the boat was teeming with people, mostly Indians.

We hadn't come all this way to see Niagara Falls over people's heads or through gaps between them. The whole idea was to get a ringside view. The regular drill of jostling my way into crowded buses while in college came in handy. I nudged past the crowd to the side of the boat and clung to the railing with both hands, till the ride was over.

As the falls got closer and closer, I became oblivious to the people around; it was all about goggling at the scene. There was that special moment when my nose almost brushed against the Falls. Well, not exactly, my nose being too small to brush against anything, but it seemed so, for the water from the Falls splashed directly on our faces, leaving us gasping with the thrill and the cold. We could glimpse the Canadian Falls and saw a boat ferrying people from the Canadian side. You could distinguish them by their red raincoats and we waved to them like little children, thrilled when they waved back.

Once the ride was done and we came ashore, we were given the choice of dumping the raincoats in a bin or taking them with us. No prizes for guessing what we did. Like any self-respecting Indian, we rolled them up, and brought them home. They came in very handy during the Kerala floods a few months later.

There were people near the Falls selling trinkets and souvenirs. I bought a bracelet from a native American at Niagara and was thrilled to pay cash. She was the first genuine non-migrant we met in the U.S. VK, normally discreet, blundered, asking her where she was from, blushed, and quickly changed the question to 'Do you live around here?' 'Yes,' she nodded her head sagely, looking like one of the solemn Indians we had seen in pictures. That ended the conversation, and VK exited, looking contrite.

We picked up a few more souvenirs from the shops and took a cab to the railway station where Amar was waiting with our bags.

We had lovely coffee at the station; in fact, the best served in cafés so far. We could make the coffee ourselves and for the price of one cup we could fill it again. This was a useful bit of knowledge I had picked up at the restaurant in Chicago. I refilled it, multiple times—for myself, for Arpitha and then for Amar. VK watched, aghast, and, unaware that his BP was rising, I asked if he'd like some. 'It would make a neat five cups. Excellent coffee,' I added, as a recommendation from one who had drunk it to the lees.

'Indians have a special knack for this,' he fumed and foamed at the mouth, as if he had taken a sip of cappuccino.

Amar took up the topic matter-of-factly and remarked that it was mostly Indians who used the returns policy offered in department stores and online chains. Rather, they misused it. At Starbucks, they made away with the newspapers.

'No sense of honour,' VK added, and prophesied that very soon, they'd ban Indians from having coffee.

'That'd be a shame,' I commented, giving Arpitha a wink. 'For the coffee is superb.'

The Amtrak station had an interesting feature—a real museum. We had some time to kill and so we decided to step inside the Niagara Falls Underground Railroad Heritage Center. As with almost all museums in the U.S., we had to pay an entrance fee but we didn't mind. For one, Amar was doing the paying, but more importantly, it was a very special museum, one that commemorated slaves who had escaped from the South and passed by Niagara en route to Canada.

The 'Underground' did not refer to what is now called the subway. No; it meant the phenomenon of thousands of slaves, fleeing the horrors of the South, taking trains to Niagara and 'going underground' or disappearing into Canada. Violence, deprivation and starvation would have been their companions, but the desire for freedom propelled people to do extraordinary things. The museum was a testimony to them and their courage.

What a smartly organised museum it was, with exhibits that brought home the reality of the underground phenomenon, and guides who were friendly without being patronising. The building we were in housed an exhibition called 'One More River to Cross', and was part of a more extensive set of places that shed light on the Underground Movement. The museum looked local and small, but opened our eyes to so much more. Our only regret was that we had a train to catch. So, after a quick dekko, we bought some souvenirs and hurried upstairs to join Amar who, after getting us tickets, was back on the platform huddled over a book on either management principles or coding or whatever techies were grilled on at job interviews.

Since this was a journey in daylight, I planned to give my complete attention to the sights outside. The Hudson River beckoned, but sleep beckoned too, and I gave in to the latter since VK's nocturnal escapades had kept us all up. The beautiful scenes of the Hudson River went by unnoticed and unappreciated, but Amar took pictures and I took consolation in those later. The train reached Syracuse on time and Deepa and Ram were at the station to pick us up. A&A left for Arpitha's house while we left with our hosts for the day.

# The Train to Poughkeepsie

DEEPA AND RAM SAW US off at Syracuse railway station the next day. They had been lovely hosts, and Nandika's company had been so refreshing, we were sorry to say goodbye. As we alighted, a cab zoomed in and A&A jumped out—perfect timing.

I called Rajive, my friend who was hosting us at Fishkill, to let him know the train was on time. Did I speak too soon? For at the station before Poughkeepsie, the train halted for ages.

VK was used to this. Back in India he was a huge fan of the railways. He had used their network regularly to chase me as I moved about the country during my stint as a management trainee with a nationalised bank. And then, for over 6 years he worked in colleges about 400 kilometres away from Thiruvananthapuram and had relied on the railways to be home every weekend. The railway guide was more of a friend and a philosopher to him than a guide. So, I was not surprised when he stepped out for a stroll and disappeared from view.

We waited, and waited but he was nowhere to be seen. I began to get worried. Amar said he'd find out. Now both were gone. Arpitha and I didn't know what was happening. VK wasn't taking our calls either. After some time, to my relief, Amar returned and said VK was talking (what else?) to the conductor. He's safe, Amar affirmed. Yes, but will he get back on the train at the right time? Unlike India where you can make a dash and leap in through any open door when the train is pulling out and reach your compartment the vestibule way, here such acrobatics are impossible. You better enter your compartment and go straight to your seat. The coaches are all closed mechanically when the train leaves the station and can be opened only at the discretion of the authorities.

The train finally began to move but VK was still missing. I panicked. Did he get left behind? It's again, not like in India, where you might be able to get a taxi and race the train to the next station. What does one do here? Who knows, maybe you could get arrested for just walking around looking lost, while actually being lost.

To our huge relief, he emerged, panting. Once he caught his breath and we began breathing easy, we asked him what had taken him so long. Here is what he said, in his voice.

'A carriage, different in looks from the ones we were riding in, attracted my attention. A sleeping car, it said! Let me wake it up. Standing close to it was a dapper, uniformed conductor. He turned out to be a warm, articulate and well-informed chap. I told him I was a tourist from India, that I was a traveller in one of the passenger coaches, and then asked him if I could take a peek inside. Sorry, he said, against the rules. You need a sleeper ticket to step inside.

'Hiding my disappointment, I asked him a few questions about the long halt and the train and then mentioned that back in India this Amtrak train would look like a toy train. "Why?" Leroy—that was his name—asked and gave me the opening I was waiting for. By now we had been joined by a few other curious passengers. I began to wax lyrical on the sheer size and scale of the railway system in India. Of the incredible numbers transported across hundreds of kilometres every day. Set up by the British, I admitted, but improved and expanded and run most efficiently by Indians. Things were not perfect. We did not have the sleek and fast trains Europe boasted of. (And which Americans could not boast of, I thought with some delight.) There were occasional delays and rare accidents, but there was nothing to beat it for stress-free, long-distance travel. Particularly if one had a reserved accommodation in a sleeper coach, I pointed out. No frills, but pretty good nevertheless.

'One of the gentlemen who had joined us now entered the conversation. "Yes", he said, "I have worked in China and Japan and travelled in Europe and most of Asia. The U.S. system is no match for what is to be found abroad."

'The gentleman's name was Steven, a retired Sheraton executive with a fascinating story. He was a Californian, had studied humanities in Stanford, joined the Sheraton group as an executive and served in many parts of the world, much of it in

Asia. I wanted to stand up and salute him when he said this but since we were all standing anyway, I confined my appreciation to some muttered phrases of appreciation. Leroy nodded at his words. "I have heard about the fast trains of Europe," he said, "but did not know that India had any kind of an efficient network."

'Steven was travelling to New York to see some plays on Broadway, a sort of annual pilgrimage, he hinted.

'The others drifted away but the three of us engaged in an earnest discussion. We were total strangers, from very different backgrounds, but we found ourselves on common ground as we talked about trains, public transport, privatisation, the duties of governments in democracies, the common good and so on. Leroy was most eloquent about some of this. He did not mention a certain blonde gentleman by name but seemed to feel personal pain at what he and his free market fundamentalist friends were doing to Amtrak and to so much more of America's public infrastructure. I was impressed not just by Leroy's attitude but also his grasp of the figures related to budgetary allocation to the public sector in his country. Wow, I thought, back home he would be on TV commenting on the railway budget.

'Steven seemed to agree with Leroy on most matters. Strange, for he was a private sector man. But he was, I soon noticed, no neoliberal in his attitudes. At one point, he turned to me and asked,

"Have you heard of Vikram Seth?" "Yes, of course, why do you ask?" I said. "Well," he mentioned with a smile, "we were friends a long time ago, in California. We stayed together for over a year." "What! You are Vikram Seth's friend?" I wanted to ask him if he had stayed with Seth or lived with him, but didn't have the nerve. Instead, I asked, "Are you in *The Golden Gate?*" He smiled again. "Read and find out."

'I did not have time to ask more questions for now Leroy grabbed my arm. "Come, I'll show you the inside of this car." I was thrilled, more by his change of attitude than what I saw inside. The inside looked more like the first-class sleeper carriage of an Indian express train. Just a corridor and the closed doors to private cabins. All the glasses were dark. "Here," said Leroy and took me to the last cubicle in the carriage. It was for the conductor, which meant it was his cubicle. He showed me the seat that could be turned into a bed, and some other features. There was even a toilet, artfully hidden beneath what appeared to be a normal seat. Every cubicle had its private toilet. Hmmm... Amtrak had scored over Indian Railways there.

'We stepped out and continued our conversation. I was so conditioned by my memories of railway platforms in India that I missed some cues indicating that my train was about to leave. Leroy and Steven quickly got into the sleeper coach. "Hurry," said Leroy as he closed his door. I looked around and saw myself on a nearly empty platform. I moved to the nearest passenger carriage and tried to open it. But this wasn't India; the door would not budge. I nearly panicked. Looking ahead, I noticed the conductor who had first met us—a tall, handsome, uniformed gentleman with dreadlocks—standing some distance away. I ran as fast as I could, remembering the warning that all passengers had to board the train a full five minutes before departure. In India such warnings were confined to the pages of the railway guide.

'"Yes?" asked the conductor as I drew up. "I am sorry," I panted. "I have a ticket for Poughkeepsie ... boarded at Syracuse ... got carried away talking to Leroy." "Leroy!" he exclaimed, then smiled and opened the door. I hurried to my seat to find K, A&A looking at me with anxious faces. "What happened? You nearly gave me a heart attack," K clutched her heart and said. As I sank into the seat beside her, I smiled sheepishly, but thought to myself, not the first time had that happened. Not the last time either, I suspect. But I told myself I needed to be a little more mindful. I took out my phone and glanced at it. There were several missed calls; from K and the two As. I felt even more sheepish. I had not heard a single one.

'Had I been left on the platform, I would have been in one hell of a spot. I had little cash, a dicey phone that worked in fits and starts, an Indian debit card that most American cash machines rejected, and no idea which way Poughkeepsie was. And, most crucially, no Amar or Arpitha to turn to for help.

'Even as we resumed our journey and I settled down to watch the scenery, I thought of what Leroy had said and remembered the museum at Niagara. And also the National Rail Museum in Delhi. It struck me that most people saw the railways in India as something the British had set up to exploit the place—to take away much of the timber and other raw material as efficiently as possible, to move troops and officials and not for any altruistic purpose. But the railways had transformed India; indeed, helped make it. If I remember right, Narendra Jadhav's *Outcaste: A Memoir* narrates the plight of the Dalits in India, much like the Blacks of the U.S., and how they had used the railways to get away from oppressive and crushing social circumstances. Travelling ticketless, starving, beaten, abused and despised, they wound up in industrial centres like Bombay and Calcutta. Here, they also, in a sense, "went underground".

'The railways followed a very enlightened policy of what the Americans called affirmative action. Many of the men and women fleeing the brutality of their villages ended up in slums beside railway tracks. Caste mattered less in urban settings, particularly if you could provide manual labour. Some found jobs with the railways. Even when the job was of the lowest type—sanitation work or the backbreaking work in the yards—it transformed their lives. There was a salary and often a "quarters" to live in. Soon, this meant schooling for their children. Countless Indian lives, I knew, were transformed by national institutions like the railways. But there were no museums to these folks in India. And the National Rail Museum in New Delhi had nothing to say about them. It was more about maharajahs and queens and viceroys. And the coaches built for them.

'But, if the railways fascinate you, the Delhi rail museum is a magical place. Leroy and Stephen, wherever you are, please visit it. It will blow your mind.'

Once VK had finished his tale, I commented, 'I'd love to see these mysterious people who held you in thrall.'

Amar smiled. 'I took a picture of them talking,' he said, selecting it from the millions in his phone, a task made simple since it was the last photo he had taken. It was a unique picture, for it had three men—one Black, one White and one Khaki—intent on one conversation. More recently, when Joe Biden was elected president, I harked back to this incident. Amtrak Joe, the first American Amtrak president. Oh, boy, Leroy, what joy this must have brought you; three cheers!

The train picked up speed and reached Poughkeepsie station on the dot—at exactly 4.48.

Rajive Joseph was waiting at the station. He was my friend from my Punjab National Bank days, and, like me, he too had quit the bank, but took the MBA route and settled in the U.S. He was now sales manager of the North

American division of Akay Spices Pvt Ltd, though he'd rather be known as the Grand Wizard of Spices. I picked up all this much later, having lost contact with him and then getting back in touch just a few years ago.

When I had told him we were coming to the U.S. for Arpitha's graduation from Syracuse University, he shouted, 'Syracuse? Syracuse?' I was pleased with the eagerness in his response until I realised he couldn't hear me well; the connectivity was poor. But he was delighted too, when I confirmed it was indeed Syracuse for it wasn't too far from where he lived. 'If you're coming to Syracuse, you have to come home. Best to take the train to Poughkeepsie.'

It was my turn to be puzzled. 'Po ... ke ... poke what? What must I come by train to poke my nose and see?'

'No, no, it's a place!' He had to shout out the spelling several times before I got it. Later we learnt he actually lived in a place called Fishkill in Dutchess County, NY. Poughkeepsie was the station where we had to alight.

What unusual names they had in the U.S., many of them taken from the languages of the indigenous native American tribes—Poughkeepsie, Wisconsin, Winnebago, Massachusetts, Skookumchuck ... Sadly, though many names had been retained, the native Americans were hardly to be seen. In fact, except for the display in the museums and a few statues, the only native American we saw was the lady selling trinkets outside Niagara Falls.

Coming back to names, there's even a place in San Bernardino County in California that actually bears, with stoicism, I'm sure, the name Zzyzx. Apparently, it had a staid name—Soda Springs—until a dubious 'doctor', Curtis Howe

Springer, sprang up with something fancy. He founded the Zzyzx Mineral Springs Resort, for he wanted it to be the last word in the English language. The American Medical Association frowned upon his pretensions and called him the 'King of Quacks'; however the quack had the last laugh, for his name for Soda Springs stuck.

But not to worry. We have our own special names for places in India, all calculated to twist the tongues of tourists into tight knots and flip them back into their throats. Ask an American to get tickets to Thiruvananthapuram, Bengaluru, Koyampuththoor, Bhubaneshwar, Dharamshala, Tiruchirappalli, Udhagamandalam (the good old Ooty), Kozhikode, Alappuzha, Mahabaleshwar, Secundrabad, and he'd decide to give India a miss. Unless he chances upon Goa. Goa with its easy, rolling off one's tongue, name is every tourist's choice of a good destination (and name). I am sure tourists would have loved it if other places in India had similarly simple names, but, alas, travellers cannot be choosers.

✦

It was great to see Rajive. He is a chap with a delightful sense of humour. Back in the day, after heavy lectures on finance and banking, credit investments and risk management at the Staff Training College, Hyderabad, we trainees would shake all those boring subjects off our befuddled heads thanks to light conversation spearheaded by Rajive.

He had met VK before but was meeting A&A for the first time. Introductions done, we hopped into his car.

Fishkill was obviously a great place to kill time, with its serene surroundings, scenic beauty and the rest of it, but during the car ride to Rajive's, we were so busy catching up, we barely noticed the sights that rolled by.

He had a lovely home and an equally lovely family— wife, daughter, mother-in-law and dog. We met his wife Deepa and daughter Kirti, both doctors, in the evening. Till they reached, I spent much of my time dodging the dog, Myna. All dogs find me irresistible, and ensure my heart is thudding permanently in my mouth when they foist their company on me.

The U.S. is perfect for long walks, and that evening we took one around the beautiful neighbourhood with our hosts, dropping in at the house of their friend, Shailaja Ledella, whom we had briefly met at Kirti's engagement in Kottayam, a city in Kerala. We rounded off a most satisfying day slurping over fried rice, mutton curry, chicken cutlets and the rest of it, while Arpitha had to satisfy herself with the vegetarian dishes. I always feel vegetarians miss out on so much, but then, they don't know what they are missing. So that's all right, I suppose.

# The Tornado

WE MEANT TO HEAD TO Roosevelt House, then a castle, and for some sightseeing along the banks of the Hudson to wind up the outing—at least that was Rajive's plan. But starting at least an hour late had become our practice from day one of our U.S. visit. Good thing we weren't on a conducted tour—we'd have been freezing our heels in hotel rooms most days, having got left behind.

By the time we were ready to leave for our day of sightseeing in Fishkill, it was 11.30. The key reason for the delay was the delicious breakfast of fresh idlis. Who wants to go to anyone's house, be it Roosevelt's or Kennedy's, when there are fluffy idlis on the breakfast table? By then it was time for Amar to take his train to New York for he had his next interview there at 4 p.m.

Rajive dropped him at the station and Amar just about beat the clock. After Rajive double-checked that he was on the right train, we left for the FDR Museum.

We keep hearing of presidential libraries and memorials all the time. I can recall at least three U.S. presidents being the butt of the same joke. This was the template. 'Did you hear, there was a fire at the White House and the president's library was reduced to ashes.' 'What? How sad.' 'Yes, both his books were burned. And he had not finished colouring one of them yet.'

This is probably more an example of the American's capacity for self-deprecation—an art at which the British are said to be masters—than the actual reading habits of U.S. presidents.

In fact, a visit to the Franklin D. Roosevelt Presidential Library and Museum will convince you of the opposite—the scholarship, leadership and vision that make a great political leader and the care and attention that have gone into preserving his heritage.

Hyde Park was just over half an hour's drive from Rajive's home at Fishkill. The memorial was in a huge estate. It was the first presidential library to be set up in the U.S. Given the number of important posts FDR held and the amount of paperwork they generated, only a big facility like FDR's old house and a library building he erected could house them.

The place is run by the National Park Service and the National Archives. There are about 50,000 books there; 23,000 of them came from FDR's personal collection. He seemed to collect books like some contemporary leaders collect selfies.

His house, Springwood, is a sprawling structure and gives us a glimpse into the man and the world he helped shape. Some of the rooms are so well maintained—preserved with the covers and carpets actually used in FDR's time—that one gets the feeling that if the great man walked in, he would feel at ease. The guides reminded us that FDR's career as president is roughly coeval with that of Adolf Hitler. But what a contrast.

It was here that the New Deal was crafted, his concept of 'four freedoms'—freedom of speech, freedom of worship, freedom from want and freedom from fear, all of which have seeped into our Constitution—was refined, meetings with international leaders were held, plans for his 'March of Dimes' charity were set up—the funding for Jonas Salk's famous polio vaccine came from this FDR baby—and so on.

Everything appeared significant. The wheelchair he had designed and the secret lift in the house touched you, as did the landscape and trees outside and FDR's grave in the compound. It was hard to believe that all this achievement was by a man who at thirty-nine was stricken by polio and could not walk or even stand without the help of heavy metal braces and needed a wheelchair to move around his own home. Though not many knew of it for he wanted his dependence on the wheelchair to be a secret, and to a great extent he was successful.

A light drizzle began as we wound up the tour with a visit to FDR's graveside.

'Let's have some food,' Rajive said, leading us to Applebee's.

The waitress there was different from others in the sense she didn't just stop with an enthusiastic greeting. She continued with an effusive conversation while taking our order and serving us. As we tucked into a late lunch, I noticed Rajive, Arpitha and VK constantly checking their phones. It wasn't like VK, at any rate, to do that, especially when engaged in conversation. What was up?

'An alert about a tornado,' VK announced, barely able to suppress his excitement. 'From 4.15 to 4.45.'

'A tornado? An actual tornado?' I couldn't believe our luck. My faith in the U.S. weather forecasters had skyrocketed after the experience at Onondaga Lake. If they issue a warning about a tornado, you can be sure it won't be a zephyr that blows instead. In India, the weather forecast continues to be as unpredictable as the weather itself.

Sure enough, at 4, dark clouds marshalled themselves together to envelope the sky, and the rain that had started as a deceptive drizzle came down in torrents. And the wind! Though we were safely ensconced in the café and couldn't hear anything, we could sense its power through the glass windows as leaves swept past in bizarre patterns, trees swayed like delicate reeds, and the rain was clearly being manipulated by the forceful winds.

Rajive was pretty amazed too. He had been in the U.S. for years and hadn't experienced a tornado, while we, mere fledgling travellers in the U.S., had been offered the spectacle of a full-blown one. 'Not fair,' he chuckled.

At this moment he got a call. It was from Kirti. Apparently, she had taken shelter during the storm at a Laundromat but the woman who ran it had objected to Myna, who was with her, and ordered her to get out. She refused. Rajive conveyed this to us, looking very nervous. He was worried his spirited daughter, having been brought up in New York, wouldn't give in. And that was exactly what happened.

When the alerts, that had continued to micro inform about the path of a storm to the last gust of wind, issued an all clear, we ventured out of the café and were confronted with the aftermath of a tornado, scenes familiarised by TV footages. We saw uprooted trees and broken branches on the roadside. Trees reclined higgledy-piggledy on houses and buildings. It took us ages to get back to Rajive's house. Power lines too had been overpowered by a superior force and the poles lay on the road in powerless submission. And then we witnessed the admirable discipline of people—in cars, that is. There were hardly any humans on the road.

At one point we were on a four-lane section, three of which were blocked by fallen trees. Vehicles clogged the road and waited their turn to take the single lane still free to accommodate traffic. There was nobody around— neither policemen nor locals—taking voluntary control, as it often happens in India. All the traffic lights were down. In the far distance we could see the flashing lights of a fire engine, helping to clear trees stretched across the road. Incredibly, drivers in all four lanes were following the zip system that Amar had familiarised us with on the first day. VK pointed this out and Rajive, worried about his daughter, but driving with restraint, agreed. 'You have to hand it to the Americans. In queues, they are great. Unless you cut in to someone else's space,' he added.

While we were still on the road, Rajive received a call from Kirti that she had stood her ground, waited there till the storm blew over and was now back on the road, with the dog. That brought the smile back on Rajive's face. 'We don't want a dead Myna,' he quipped.

We watched Rajive let a car full of New Yorkers pass. When VK remarked, 'That's very kind of you,' Rajive laughed. 'Not really, it was more fear for my life. You never know who has a shotgun under their seat. They shoot first and apologise later. I play it safe.' Gun ho!

We had to take the 7.15 Amtrak that evening. The traffic had still not returned to normal and we were sure we'd miss the train. But we reached the station at 7.13 to find that trains had not been running since 4 p.m. Deepa had warned us about this likelihood and had tried hard to persuade us to stay back. But we never believed there'd be any problem; after all this was the U.S. When she realised we were determined to be foolish, she had done the next best thing—packed dinner for us. Rajive was waiting outside the station and called to say he'd take us back home. But we continued to be optimistic and when Arpitha got a message on her phone from Amtrack that our train would arrive at 8.55, we thought it made sense to wait. We asked Rajive to go back home.

There were a few other hopefuls at the station. But the man at the information counter was extremely unhelpful. For the first time since our arrival, I encountered rude behaviour. I asked him, 'Excuse me, sir, when will the train arrive?' He just shook his head and mumbled, 'Aw. Don't know.' VK went to try his luck, but he nodded grimly and shrugged his shoulders, tight-lipped. When Arpitha went a little later, he turned his head away.

Since I had received the best response, VK and Arpitha sent me once again to the counter. This time, he repeated, 'I don't know,' adding very sternly 'and please don't come back with the same question.' Had this happened in India, where delays are a constant, we'd have been much better informed by now. And people tell you what they know, not withhold basic information as if they would divulge a state secret by opening their mouths.

When I returned, tail between legs, VK was talking to a woman, who I later learnt, was Jamaican and worked in the travel industry. She was very indignant when she heard my story. 'How could he.' She breathed out some fire and hoisted her bag on her shoulder.

My heart warmed to her. 'Spunky lady, she's going to give the chap a piece of her mind.'

'I'm leaving,' she announced. 'I don't think there's any point waiting.' And the spunky lady marched out of the station.

'She calls herself Jamaican but hasn't even heard of Michel Holding,' VK rued.

But we continued to be hopeful. Train cancellations, with no notice, couldn't happen in a First World country, surely? But they could, and they did. We soon understood that the U.S. is so used to nothing going wrong that it is caught napping when something does. The Third World, so disaster-centric, is much better equipped to deal with crises. At 9, we had dinner on a bench on the platform. That felt like home. We saw a conductor walk past and wondered if he'd have any information for us. As it turned out, he was more helpful. He said that though there was no official confirmation, he was certain all trains had been cancelled for the day.

Rajive called to say he'd come to pick us up and a little abashed, we went outside the station to wait for him. We felt very bad about the trouble our stubborn faith in the

U.S. system had brought him. As we waited, we watched the few people still there finding ways to return home or taking cabs to NY. We were asked by a couple of people if we wanted a lift but we declined. We began to get a little frightened too; the station was beginning to look deserted and scary. All those stories of mugging, all those thrillers we'd seen, began to play on our minds.

A man who was going towards a car that had pulled up, abruptly turned on his heels and came to us. We froze. 'I don't think it's safe to remain here. Find some way to leave,' he advised, before returning to his ride. Nice man, but I could only respond with a nervous nod. Nodding was, anyway, the preferred method of communication at the station. A large Black woman who was part of a group came up to say it wasn't wise to wait there. 'Want a lift?' 'No, thank you very much,' I shook my head vigorously. Another group that was trying to organise people to hire a vehicle to go to New York asked if we were interested. I nodded my head side to side, exhausting my language of nods. VK chipped in to say, 'Someone is coming for us. Thanks.'

Soon we were the only ones at that eerie station and when Rajive arrived, we greeted him as if he was rescuing us from a caved-in mine. When we returned to his house, not one member of his family said, 'We told you so.' Myna welcomed me with a whoop and I responded with a hoop backwards.

Before we went to sleep, totally drained out, Amar called to say he had just managed to beat the tornado. He had been able to attend his interview and did it 'okay'. And he also managed to get the refund from Amtrack.

Train services were restored by morning and Arpitha booked fresh tickets. Rajive dropped us at the Poughkeepsie North Metro Station, rather close to the Amtrak station which looked so cheerful and normal in the morning, it was hard to believe it had scared the hell out of us the previous night. And the roads too looked as if the tornado had never been. Wah, America!

# New York

THE TRAIN LEFT ON TIME and we alighted at Grand Central Station. Yes, we were in New York—the Big Apple, the first capital of the U.S., the city that never sleeps, nicknamed Metropolis by day and Gotham by night, the beloved muse for so many writers, formerly New Amsterdam before the British renamed it after the Duke of York. It gave us a wet welcome.

It was raining and we thought it made sense to buy an umbrella. The umbrellas we had brought from India were safe in our suitcases, like our gloves. There was a Black man selling umbrellas at the entrance and while waiting for the cab, we bought one. 'Five dollars,' he said. Arpitha selected a card from among the many hanging down her wrist, but the man said, 'No, ma'am, cash, please. We are poor people.' He said this without a trace of self-pity. I was moved, and delighted. Moved by his response and delighted I could finally use the cash I had with me. Amar had given me notes of different denominations during his last visit and I hadn't been able to use any, for the card holders always managed to get in first.

I whipped out my wallet and gave him five dollars. And

he gave me a million-dollar smile, dazzling white teeth and all. As we got into the cab, I saw a policeman hustle him off. Unperturbed, he gathered his Chinese-made umbrellas in a box and shuffled away. Clearly there was precarious livelihood here too but there was a dignity to him that touched me.

We got a taste of proper urban living in New York— busy roads, bustling people, cosmopolitan crowds, towering skyscrapers, colourfully lit up streets, commercial areas, the yellow taxi ... But what got my goat was the iconic but totally confusing New York City subway. It's a great way to get around, or so it's touted, but for me it was all about playing Mary's little lamb to my tech-savvy son and daughter-in-law.

We started with the good old Uber, though, taking one from the station to Harrison in New Jersey where Amar was waiting for us in a comfortable suite at, well, Comfort Suites. Why doesn't some eccentric businessman give names like 'Cramped Spaces', 'Intolerable Inn', 'Dismal Dungeon' or 'Hellish Hovel' to their posh hotel chains? It would provide the charm of suspense and excitement to the process of selecting hotel accommodation.

My first subway experience was the train journey from New Jersey to Penn station that afternoon. Amar did his usual peering into the phone to get touching results. We walked up two flights of steps to reach the sleek platform. A train had just pulled in and we got into one of its cars.

'We get off at Penn station,' Amar said as we got in. 'And I'm getting off with you.' Pen, Pencil, Gift-wrap Paper or Penpwppepowepne, nothing mattered as long as I could alight with him. These subway trains made me nervous.

The train started almost immediately and I realised you had to be very alert and agile if you had to board and get off at the right stations. That thought raised my BP, or, rather, made it normal for I have low BP. The crowded train soon went subterranean and we stood, hanging on to the straps, stress levels rising, nothing but darkness outside, stuck with a lot of unsmiling people.

At the first stop, I asked a dour man of Indian origin, who stood nearby, what station it was.

'Sshh!' he put a finger to his lips like a stern school marm, pointing to a sign that said, 'Silent'. I hadn't realised this was a silent compartment and I went red with embarrassment. The stuffed shirt looked smug; his good deed for the day was done and dusted. He strutted to an exit, all ready to be the first to alight at the next stop.

A sympathetic glance from an American man standing across made me feel better. But I felt best when the train stopped and the Indian found, to his chagrin, that the platform was on the other side. He rushed to the opposite exit that already had a lot of people waiting, caught his bag on something and caught my eye when he exclaimed, 'What the...!' I put my finger to my lips. He was the last to get off, lips set in a grim line. The quiet American winked.

At the station, we hovered around Amar who was figuring out which exit to take, since every exit led to a different street, when a bustling Indian man shouted at us to get out of his way in Hindi—'Hato, hato!' Two rude people in one afternoon, and both Indians.

Getting out into the right street and with the rain, our faithful friend, for company, we took just five minutes to walk from Penn to the Empire State Building, in effect, the New York Building, for Empire State is yet another nickname of NY.

Willis Tower might be taller than the Empire State Building, but the latter, with its individualistic, elegant design—at least as elegant as any skyscraper can be—and iconic status, is in a class of its own.

When someone was asked to say three words about the Empire State Building, pat came the answer, 'Tallest building, America, King Kong.' Wrong on a couple of counts and exceeded the word limit too. It's no longer the tallest building and is in the U.S., not a vague America. The third choice was the most revealing. *King Kong* is a 1933 film, yet the image of the giant gorilla going up the Empire State Building has been passed down from generation to generation. People remember the airplanes shooting down the fictitious King Kong, but the tragic actual crashing of a U.S. bomber plane into the 79th floor at the end of World War II was recalled only when 9/11 happened. Such is the defining power of cinema.

The queue at the entrance wasn't as long as the one to get into Willis Tower—the height of a building probably determines the length of the queue—but it included a lot of Indians. We found our fellow countrymen at all the key touristy spots—Willis Tower, Niagara Falls, Empire State Building, Statue of Liberty, Boston's Aquarium—but hardly any at the museums or on university tours. Food for thought, that.

Clearing security, we were soon in the super-fast elevator that whooshed us into the glass-enclosed observation deck on the 86th floor of this 102-storied skyscraper. As we got off, I heard someone say, 'You can see five U.S. states if the sky is clear.'

'Ha! You'd be lucky to see the state of your nose,' I retorted under my breath, for it was foggy outside. But I was mistaken. If it was a drizzle that had lent mystery to the view from Willis, the misty rain and the accompanying fog made this one out of the world. The fog kept changing shape, enticing the skyscrapers around to play hide and seek with us and making the city that suffers from insomnia look quite dreamy. The Hudson River in the distance appeared to say, 'Now you see me, now you don't', and drew us into this enthralling game. I looked for and finally spotted the attractive Chrysler Building with which the Empire State Building had been engaged in a storey-to-storey battle for the title of the tallest building.

Satiated, we turned to pick up a few souvenirs. The Black man who was billing the items, beamed at us. 'Do you like Sushmita Sen?'

I thought I hadn't heard right. He drawled and drooled, 'Sushmita Sen, the Indian beauty,' he added an enthusiastic nod.

Amazed, I nodded too, and he got so lost in thoughts of her he ended up billing us twice for the same items. But his error didn't set off any electronic alarm. It was the very human Arpitha who discovered the mistake and he apologised as profusely as if Arpitha was Sushmita herself.

'It's time for Times Square,' said Amar. By the time we left the Empire State Building, it was late evening, and as we walked towards Times Square, I felt as if Wisconsin was light years away. We had stepped into a bright new world of noise, crowds, neon lights, colourful billboards, street performers, theatres, restaurants, shops ... and it still rained.

'Hey, look who's here,' VK exclaimed and whom did we see reclining nonchalantly against two waste disposal bins on the roadside but a Donald Trump lookalike—orange face, yellow whipped-up hair, and that typical disgruntled expression. The well-fed figure wore a fancy suit with a striped tie, and beside him an open volume of Hillary Clinton's memoir, *What Happened*, was propped up. There was a tumbler near it labelled 'Wall Fund'. What a cool way to beg! We dropped a couple of notes in; the novel method deserved a reward. I was struck by the self-respect with which people requested charity in the U.S. There is no one persistently scratching your elbow, tugging at your sleeve or bag, chanting 'Give, give' as it happens in India. Contribution is voluntary. People dress up, perform or play music, some just walk about carrying placards that announce a heart-tugging, 'I am hungry.' And you give.

In the beginning it was enjoyable—the feel of being in Times Square in the mild fog and drizzle—but after a bit, the chill seeped into my bones.

'Any place where we can find shelter?' I asked Amar, hugging my arms.

'How about there? Or there?' Amar gestured to the left. And, believe it or not, there they were, Madame Tussauds and Ripley's, practically next door to each other.

'Ripley's, of course.' I was excited, not feeling the cold any longer. Who wants to see wax models when an unbelievable world beckoned? Familiar with Ripley's 'Believe it or Not' offerings, I had always been fascinated by the man who had been voted more popular than President Roosevelt by *The New York Times* and who holds the record for receiving the most letters in history. VK must come a close second; I wrote him any number.

One of my favourite Ripley cartoons is of the Chinese American baby born the day of Lindberg's trans-Atlantic flight and named by his parents, One Long Hop. Whether he turned into a compulsive flyer, long jumper or a frog is anyone's guess. Robert Ripley had a huge following, though many chose to be sceptical of his claims and called him, 'The Biggest Liar in the World'. He wore the title with pride, secure in the knowledge that he was right.

The tickets to enter Ripley's were a rip off, but you have to pay through the nose to see the man with the golden one. We spent the next hour in the odditorium, gaping at a car tyre gorilla, a car parts Captain America, shrunken heads, peculiar skeletons, a two-headed sheep, a cow with six legs, a man with a forked tongue and similar bizarre exhibits. We entered the black hole with screaming children for company, walked on water, stood near the tallest man, sat with a Native American and a long-necked Burmese woman, and gazed in ghoulish wonder at 'The Criminal Mind'—half the head of an eighteenth century French criminal, preserved, so the caption said, 'Because a criminal mind is a terrible thing to waste.'

At the torture chamber, Amar and VK got transformed into excited ten-year-olds, examining cruel instruments of torture like The Iron Maiden we had only read about. They 'enjoyed' the experience of being in the pillory and wearing the heavy chains and metal helmets that had entwined and encased condemned prisoners in medieval times. Who would have imagined they harboured these ghoulish aspirations.

'Arpitha, where do we put our heads?' I asked, feeling left out.

'There, Aunty.' She pointed to a couple of pickled heads. We promptly stuck our heads into empty jars kept near them so it looked like our heads were pickled too. Tickled by the pickled experience, we took pictures to frighten the wits out of friends.

But what was Marilyn Monroe's driving licence doing at Ripley's? Maybe Ripley wished to say, 'Believe it or not, ladies and gentlemen, blondes can drive, and here's proof.'

Once we had our fill of extraordinary, jaw-dropping stuff, we felt the need to get our jaws working and fill our hungry stomachs. It was still drizzling as we walked along Broadway and came to Hard Rock Café.

Hard Rock blazed a name board with 'Love All Serve All' painted below it. Some tennis aficionado must have thought up that motto. When the café is closed, they probably changed it to, 'Service Over. Love All.'

'How about a taste of Hard Rock?' Amar asked.

'Tough to digest,' VK grinned. 'But, why not?'

'Hey, the Beatles,' I exclaimed, pleased to see the picture of my favourite rock band amongst the rock and roll memorabilia mounted on the walls while we waited to be allowed in. A young man soon arrived to lead us to our table to the accompaniment of ear-blasting rock music.

'Part of the ambience of Hard Rock.' Amar looked

apologetically at VK, but VK was already shaking his head to the beat. He has strange taste in music that ranges from soothing classical stuff to the hardest rock composed specifically to take your head apart.

We couldn't hear one another talk but managed to place our order. I had a bad throat and wanted hot water.

'No. This is Hard Rock Café,' VK said as if it explained all.

'You won't get it here,' Arpitha clarified in words of one syllable. She added, 'No one asks for hot water, Aunty.'

'No one drinks it,' Amar added. 'Ask for normal water, room temperature.'

But I knew what that would mean. Americans have a problem with temperature as they have with size. Normal water for them is iced water and cold water is iced water with icebergs big enough to sink two Titanics floating on top.

'Hot water, please,' I appealed to the friendly, pony-tailed chap waiting on us, to the embarrassment of all. I indicated my throat and mouthed, 'Sore throat,' hoping he could lip read.

The dumb charade worked. He looked concerned. 'Hot water?' He danced a small jig as if he had stepped on hot bricks. 'We have very hot water ready for tea. Will that do?'

I nodded eagerly. He brought a jug full of boiling hot water, and guess what? Everyone at my table wanted some too to bring their iced water to normal. Ha!

It was 12.30 when we returned, dog tired, having taken a bus and a cab to get back to the hotel.

Arpitha was in total charge the next day, Amar staying

back for some work. She had booked us on the 12.30 Statue of Liberty cruise. This left the forenoon free; so off we went by train to Penn station from where we walked to Madison Square Garden.

Madison Square Garden is neither square nor a garden. Nor is it in Madison. It's a round indoor sports arena in the heart of New York City, one of the world's most famous stadiums, known universally for having hosted the 'Fight of the Century' world heavy weight championship clash between Muhammed Ali and Joe Frazier in 1971. The mutual animosity of the legendary boxers continued way beyond their boxing careers, fuelled mostly by Ali shooting his mouth off. When Frazier was asked for his comments on Ali lighting the cauldron at the 1996 games, he is believed to have snapped, 'They should have pushed him in.'

Sports fans throng MSG to watch their favourite NBA and NHL teams, other popular sports, music concerts and special events. A fascinating feature of MSG is the way the settings are changed to suit the games being hosted. An ice hockey rink is transformed into a basketball court or a boxing ring, and equally deftly gets readied for the next ice hockey game. Nothing short of magic, if you don't know how it is done.

To our huge disappointment, we had to settle for a cursory look from the outside since it was getting prepared for the graduation ceremony of the students of one of the CUNY (City University of New York) colleges. A few students in their purple gowns bustled about.

'Can't we take just one glimpse of the concave ceiling of MSG?' I wanted to peer in. I had heard so much about the unusual panelled ceiling, the only one of its kind in the world, and the only part of the arena that stays untouched.

'Not possible, Aunty.' Arpitha shook her head.

'I think we have to make do with looking at these students,' VK said with a wry smile.

'And they are not even concave. Or convex. Plain shapeless in their gowns,' I mourned as we left the place.

Madison Square Garden's loss was Central Park's gain for we headed there to grace it with our dishevelled presence, broken umbrellas and all. It was hard to believe that this delightful urban oasis, New York's answer to Europe's famed public parks, was originally a muddy swamp full of rocks. Money, clean water and topsoil were poured into it. The story goes that more gunpowder was used to blast and clear out the rocks there than by soldiers during the Battle of Gettysburg.

As light, wispy rain fell, we strolled under the canopy of lush, intertwining trees along the clean, winding walkways that had old street lamps lining them. Sparrows chirped on the grass. Strolling along the bridge over a lake, we saw ducks swimming lazily in the water. Holden Caulfield need not have had panic attacks obsessing over where they would go in winter, for, wherever they went, I bet they always returned like homing pigeons to Central Park in spring.

'Now for Cleopatra's Needle,' said VK. I hate to disappoint those who imagine this is something exotic, for the name Cleopatra promises nothing less. It is special, all right, but there is nothing glamorous about a 3,000-year-old Egyptian Obelisk that had found a home in Central Park. Its antique value cannot be disputed—it is the oldest outdoor monument in NY City.

We noticed many people walking their dogs, among whom was a lady with a dog whose leg was in a plaster cast. Arpitha loves dogs and immediately went on her knees to pet it, an act guaranteed to win over any dog owner.

'I adopted this dog from a distress home,' the lady said, smiling benignly at Arpitha. 'I found it had a broken leg when I brought it home. She's a sweetie, no trouble at all.'

The sweetie took the cue and pooped. 'Oh, the dear.' The lady took it in her stride and into her gloves with the same air of performing a sacred act that I had seen in other dog lovers in America. The gloves with the crap went into a trash can. The U.S. was certainly dog's own country. Love me, love my dog, love my dog poo.

She said she was an artist who lived in an apartment close by. 'But I'll never put up my art on social media,' she emphasised.

We had been hunting for Shakespeare Garden that was believed to have the plants and flowers mentioned in Shakespeare's plays. I looked forward to seeing Ophelia's flowers—rosemary, pansy, fennel, columbine, rue, daisy, violet—but even my acute sense of smell didn't lead us to the right place. We asked the lady who gave us very specific directions. We began to smile gratefully when she said, 'But it's closed now. Some trees are being trimmed.'

'Really?' VK's face fell.

'Yes,' she beamed. 'Very unfortunate; I'm so sorry. For this is the right time. Spring is when it's at its best—lush, lively, lovely,' she added, rubbing it in.

'Bye. Have a great time.' She resumed her walk, her dog hopping on three legs. Strange are the ways of dog lovers, they walk their injured pets for exercise.

It was time to keep our date with the guide for the Statue of Liberty tour and we took an Uber to Battery Park. The Uber driver was a Pakistani—a Trump admirer who had been in the U.S. for thirty years. He pointed out the Trump hotel with the enthusiasm with which a cab driver in Mumbai had indicated the Arthur Road Jail to us and reeled off with pride the names of the celebrities it had hosted.

The cabbie, a microbiologist who had given up the subject to become a failed businessman, was now driving an Uber to make ends meet.

'I'm learning to invest smartly,' he grinned. 'I'll soon get back my money.' He may have been short of cash, but he was certainly not short on optimism.

VK introduced cricket into the conversation and the driver smacked his lips recalling the days when Imran Khan used to make Indian batsmen shiver. 'Let Imran Khan become prime minister, and all will be well.' The world is still waiting.

*

At Battery Park we took the ferry to Liberty Island, after the mandatory security screening.

'Give me liberty or give me death,' Patrick Henry, one of America's founding fathers, had said in 1775. The British obliged, though grudgingly, with liberty; they didn't want murder on their hands, but the friendly French, who are known to add a touch of class to their generous overtures, gifted something that symbolised freedom for the

Americans—the Statue of Liberty. Liberty was the recurring theme all the way for us—Miss Liberty, the ferry, took us to Liberty Island at the mouth of Hudson River so we could take a close look at the Statue of Liberty, modelled on Libertas, the Roman goddess of liberty.

The enthusiastic guide took us around and at the start, he had the whole pack following him, hanging on his lips, metaphorically speaking. Pointing to the statuesque statue that looked as if someone had draped a saree carelessly about her, he said, 'Oxidation made the brown copper statue turn green.'

'Not envy,' guffawed a visitor, and we all laughed loudly for we had been starved of levity.

The guide smiled. 'She's tough. She's open to the elements, and gets struck by lightning bolts regularly, but stays up there, torch and tablet intact.' What a sport.

'Let's go into the statue,' the guide said and I giggled, reminded of a Woody Allen quote: 'My love life is terrible. The last time I was inside a woman was when I visited the Statue of Liberty.'

We had pedestal tickets and took the steps to reach the museum inside the statue. Everything you wish to know about the statue is there—in photos, sketches, videos and diagrams. The original 1886 torch and full-scale copper replicas of the foot and the face of the statue grabbed our attention and a few tourists grabbed the nose. Pointing to the face, the guide explained, 'The French sculptor Bartholdi made this in the likeness of his mother, Charlotte.'

'Grim lady,' someone grimaced.

'She doesn't give that impression when we see her from a

distance, but up close, she is rather fearsome,' I commented, joining the touching group to caress her nose that was shinier than the rest of her face.

'That's how most mothers are, up close.' VK winked at Amar.

I made a face and laughed, continuing to rub her nose.

'Are you soothing her ruffled feathers or is this also part of the Niels Bohr luck principle?' VK asked. Now it was his turn to make a face.

'Niels Bohr, Uncle,' Arpitha grinned, also going for the nose. 'Everyone does it. That's why the colour has changed. And Aunty, don't give the wish away.'

'Same wish, anyway,' I said. Arpitha groaned.

A few tourists who had crown tickets went on to climb all the way to the top, but the rest of us spent some more time admiring the view before descending.

Ellis Island situated nearby was part of the cruise deal and the ferry now took us there. It might look unassuming in terms of size but it is one of the most historically significant places in the U.S. Ellis Island, the Gateway to the New World, served as a federal immigration station from 1892 to 1954 and helped bring the American Dream to fruition for millions of hopeful immigrants.

It was known earlier by self-explanatory names like Gull Island, Oyster Island and Gibbet Island before a New York merchant, Samuel Ellis, purchased it in the eighteenth century and called it Oyster Island. But when it changed hands a few times to finally become the property of the federal government, it came to be called Ellis Island, after its last private owner. Nobody could think of anything better and it remains so to date. Americans have an endearingly naive attitude towards names.

The guide described all this but by then, the flock trailing him had thinned considerably. To give him credit, he was a true professional, remaining as enthusiastic as if he was Pied Piper, and to his audience of, well, just the three of us, he narrated the story of U.S. immigration as he took us around the evocative National Museum of Immigration.

The experience left us introspective and quiet, but when the cruise came to an end, we didn't forget to tip the guide handsomely as Amar had tutored us.

From Battery Park we walked to Wall Street and sighted the iconic Charging Bull. We'd have loved to charge towards it but didn't, out of fear for our lives—we were on the other side of the busy road. Also, there was an admiring crowd around it. The Charging Bull is as much of a tourist attraction as the Statue of Liberty. Even from a distance, it exuded the raw energy and belligerence its Italian American sculptor, Arturo di Modica, meant it to radiate. It appeared to be almost stumbling over in its eagerness to butt someone.

The Charging Bull was sculpted by Modica to represent the resilience and strength of Americans and up their spirits after the 1987 Black Monday Wall Street crash. He took two years over it, and by the time it was completed, the Americans had recovered their confidence, and probably some of their money, but they embraced the Charging Bull wholeheartedly as a symbol of their prosperity and optimism. We had heard that certain intimate parts of it were constantly rubbed by people so that luck would rub off on them, but Arpitha and I weren't able to, and might have hesitated to apply the Niels Bohr principle this time, to VK's great relief.

'All bull!' he commented.

Facing the Charging Bull was the bronze statue of The Fearless Girl surrounded by a group clicking selfies with it. The work of the American sculptor Kristen Visbal, The Fearless Girl adopted a fearless stance, head back, chin up, arms akimbo, appearing to throw a challenge to the Charging Bull. The statue, regarded as the symbol of women's empowerment, had been placed there the day before International Women's Day in 2017. We learnt later that after protests, especially from Modica who felt the spunky girl trivialised his creation, it was shifted in November 2018 to its present location outside the New York Stock Exchange.

Our visit to One World Trade Center in Lower Manhattan, NY City, was a sobering experience. It was impossible not to recall the disturbing images of the planes crashing into the twin towers of the World Trade Center as we approached the impressive structure that stood in their place. It was overwhelming, to be actually standing where a horrific, epic and history-changing disaster had occurred.

It filled us with a deep sense of awe, that Ground Zero, the 16 acre 70 foot deep hole of rubble, dust, and mangled steel that the attacks had reduced the twin towers to, had been replaced by this sleek building that is now the tallest in the US, and the 9/11 Memorial and Museum. If the Charging Bull is a tribute to the optimism and prosperity of the Americans, the august Memorial Tower, the serene water-themed 9/11 memorial with the names of the dead inscribed on its bronze parapets, and the remarkable museum underground, with the artefacts of the tragedy, are a testimony to their indefatigable spirit and a fitting answer to the destructive intent of the perpetrators of 9/11.

We crossed over to look for the subway station and discovered, to our embarrassment, that it was actually in The Oculus, the mammoth white structure adjacent to the Ground Zero memorial. We hurriedly re-crossed and entered the intriguing building that resembled a huge white bird about to take wing or prepare to touch down.

'Oculus' is Latin for 'eye' and in architecture refers to an eye-like opening into the sky. The Oculus, the World Trade Center Transportation Hub, takes its name from the row of skylights along the spine of its roof, and its standout design is unique in the neighbourhood of mostly rectangular skyscrapers. Architect Santiago Calatrava wanted to create something that would be 'a witness of belief that we can overcome this tragedy' and a gift 'given to the community'.

We entered this 'gift' and were instantly reduced to insignificance in its awe-inspiringly colossal, ribbed and pristine white interior. It was dotted with up end shops and we window-shopped from a respectable distance before we took the escalator down to the subway station and I felt lost and jittery immediately. But Arpitha was there and she managed the show. We took the right train to New Jersey, and then a cab to our hotel where Amar was waiting for us, looking a little anxious.

Stations in the U.S. had this effect on me, and later VK confessed that was how he had felt too. If we hadn't had Amar or Arpitha with us during our train journeys, I'm sure our nervous behaviour and suspicious movements would have landed us in the police station multiple times.

I remember at one subway station we had to insert the ticket into a slot before we could enter the platform. The machine grabbed it from me. Alarmed, I snatched it back. Amar laughed and explained that the machine would pull the ticket in and return it, not to worry. At another station, we had to swipe the pass for the barricade to open, but when I swiped, a message saying, 'You are too slow', popped up. 'All right, Usain Bolt,' I muttered and after a few frustrating attempts, my effort finally met with its stringent standards.

VK was all eager to go to the Metropolitan Museum of Art, the Met for short, the next day and so was I. Imagine going to New York and not managing a visit to the largest and the best-known museum in the U.S. But that was what happened. I woke up with a bad back and aching legs. And a visit to a museum needs indefatigable legs. The spirit was willing but the limbs were weak.

Arpitha wasn't feeling too great either, so she stayed back too, but booked a cab for her father-in-law to the Met, with strict instructions that he should call her if he needed anything. It was prepaid, so VK just had to alight in style once he reached. VK left with a spring in his step. There's no place he loves being in more than a museum.

This time the Uber driver was Mexican, a very contented Mexican too, who said his name was Junior. And VK, as usual, struck up a conversation with him that lasted the half hour it took to reach the museum. Junior confessed to him that he had run away as a teenager to the U.S. Had he stayed back in Mexico, he'd have had to join either the army or the mafia. He couldn't make it to the army, and probably decided not to give the mafia a shot; so he came to the U.S., and realised he had made the right choice. He had three flats in Mexico, two kids, one wife and one home in the U.S.

Is it true, he asked VK, that Indians had 'arranged marriages'? What is caste and what role did it play in marriage? VK said he struggled to give easy-to-understand explanations of these quintessentially Indian practices, taking some time over 'compatibility of star signs', a concept that intrigued Junior. As they parted at the Met, Junior smiled at VK and told him he loved Indian food. VK said he took that as a comment not on Indian food but on arranged marriages.

Amar had his next interview—the final one—that day. Now that Bed and Bath were done, it had to be the Beyond bit. I wondered what lay beyond Beyond. He returned after the interview with a broad smile and the mandatory, 'It was okay.' I remembered my wish and hoped he'd make it.

VK hadn't called at all, and at 6.30, Amar and I left to pick him up from the Met. I stuck to Amar like a leech during the two train journeys that were followed by two cab rides, and I stepped into the famous yellow cab for the first time; what a thrill.

At the Met, I gave a call to VK who sounded almost disappointed we had reached and was quite reluctant to come out. We sat on the steps outside, and waited, quite certain we were going to miss each other. Everything looked set for a scene of 'Where are you?' 'I'm here!' 'Where is here?' But, miracles happen. He came out, was spotted and we met, right in front of the Met. He appeared full of beans, though he had had only an apple the entire day. Amar insisted on a proper dinner and we took another yellow cab to a peaceful Indian restaurant, 'Om', before heading home, or, rather, the hotel.

We were taking the bus early next morning for Boston. Before we left the room, I snatched the pen on the table and shoved it into my bag. 'A souvenir,' I explained to VK whose eyebrows had disappeared into his hairline. 'Look, it's got "Comfort Suites" branded on it,' I comforted him.

'Put it back,' he objected, reacting as if I was showing distinct signs of kleptomania.

'What's the big deal?' I countered. 'It's only a pen.'

'I'm sure it is, for us. For them it's part of the decor of the room.'

'Look what else it says on it.' I read out, '"Rested. Set. Go." The pen has rested enough. Get set to go. I'm sure the hotel wants us to take it.'

I shoved the pen deeper into my bag, adding, 'Know what? Because of your octopus drama, I forgot to take the pen from Candlewood. I love to collect souvenirs from every place we stay.'

VK gave a telling snort. 'It's good chairs and tables are difficult to spirit away.'

# To Boston and Walden Pond

IT WAS RAINING WHEN WE checked out and we decided to take a cab to the bus stop. As always, VK began a conversation with the cabbie, an extremely nice person, who was only too pleased to open up. It was amazing how almost all the cab drivers were very forthcoming about their life stories. I had always believed that this garrulousness, especially about one's personal life, was a uniquely Indian trait.

This driver hailed from Kazakhstan. Lack of job prospects back home had brought him to the U.S., a move he didn't regret. He was happy making money driving a car in a strange land, often working fifteen hours a day. He had tried working in a warehouse first, but after two heart-stopping encounters with men brandishing drawn guns, had shifted his residence to a flat near Comfort Suites and started driving for Uber. Life was good, he said. It would have been better if his family had moved to the States, but they preferred to live in Kazakhstan.

As we reached New York's Megabus pick-up point, the cabbie became very concerned about the heavy rain. The bus stop had no shelter and the bus hadn't arrived. 'You'll get wet,' he stated the obvious and actually took a U-turn to drop us off in front of a tall office building. He advised us to take our luggage in and wait as he waved us a reluctant goodbye. His heart was in the right place all right. In my experience, cabbies don't generally do this sort of thing. They are paid to take us a particular distance, and will disgorge us even if it is beside a waste dump.

We stumbled in, wet and uncomfortable, pushing big suitcases awkwardly. A well-dressed gentleman immediately swept us out with his tongue and several 'No, no, no, no, no's with the efficiency of a good broom sweeping out dust.

American buildings lack eaves under which one can hope for some protection from the elements. Standing flat against the wall, as if lined up for the firing squad, didn't help. VK and I propped ourselves with great difficulty on the narrow strip of ground outside the building, keen on protecting at least our heads from the cold New York spring rain, while the good people inside the building watched the circus act. I hope it brightened their day.

A&A took most of our luggage across the street to join a few others waiting there, hoping to manage an early entry into our coach when it drew up. The cold, the rain, the several things we had to lug or carry, all compounded the problem. This is among the worst things about travel—managing multiple bags, a coat or a jacket on one's arm, a tote bag on one's shoulder, a phone to be kept dry and handy and the narrow confines of a plane or bus aisle to negotiate. Very good arguments for staying at home, VK averred, balanced on one foot.

A&A soon hailed us; the bus had arrived. It was a

double-decker. We climbed to the second deck—a habit from childhood days. To look down from those er ... Olympian heights and watch the world go by gives a great feeling of satisfaction. I got a window seat with VK by my side. A&A sat a few rows ahead. Having got wet in the rain, and feeling cold, my immediate concern was how I'd manage the long journey of four hours without going to the toilet. I watched everyone like a hawk, to see if all had obedient bladders.

Soon I caught sight of two women going down the steps. Where were they going when the bus hasn't stopped? Surely it wouldn't be just to stretch their legs or to take a look at the seats below? Was this their first trip on a double-decker? They were robust women and didn't look the sort who would leave their seats to seek another spot unless they had a solid motive. My curiosity roused, I kept my eyes focussed on the steps. What goes down in a moving double-decker bus must certainly come up. I wasn't wrong. Soon they returned, looking happy—or, rather, ha-pee.

I whispered my suspicion to VK that there could be a toilet on the lower deck. VK went to scout and soon returned, looking pleased. I went down and expecting something smelly, I took care not to breathe in. Odoriferous toilets might be more effective than yoga to help you learn how to hold your breath. I found a tiny boxlike place and a small toilet inside—more a hole than a toilet, but, holy moly! It was very clean. The blue water in it probably kept it so and chased the smell away.

Now I was more comfortable and, fortified with occasional snacks of yogurt and fruit raided from the fridge after breakfast at Comfort Suites, I tried to sleep but failed for a squeaky-voiced Chinese-American man in the seat before us talked non-stop into his phone all the way to Boston. If I had understood the language, at least I could have eavesdropped and got some idea of what Chinese-Americans are concerned about during bus journeys, but it was all 'Chin cho chu chem. Su me yu ...' to me.

It rained for the greater part of the journey and from the wide glass windows of the top deck, we got hazy views of thick woods, stretches of wilderness interspersed with occasional water bodies and rocky terrain, but it was mostly vehicles that we passed for we were on a busy four-lane highway. We reached Boston at 11.45 a.m.

We were staying with Luckshmi, a former student of mine, in Boston. I gave her a call and handed the phone to my son, that's how easy travelling with A&A was. Following her instructions, Amar, who was quite familiar with Boston, found the right trains to reach Alewife. What an intriguing name. Sounded pretty fishy. It was. Literally. I found out later it had been named after the nearby Alewife Brook that got its name from 'alewife', a fish. How disappointingly tame! It would have been so much more stimulating if it had been named after the perennially tipsy wife of a tavern-keeper.

Luckshmi's husband, Anil, met us at the station and drove us to their house in Lexington where she and her kids, Malavika and Madhav, were waiting for us. How lovely it was to meet them on U.S. soil. We caught up with them over a very tasty and elaborate Kerala lunch that Luckshmi had prepared for us. Sleep ought to have been the natural sequel to that very satisfying meal, but the great Walden

Pond beckoned, and its greatest votary, VK, beckoned frantically to us to get ready. Luckshmi asked us to go ahead; they would join us later. Walden Pond was just a ten-minute drive from her house.

'Lucky Luckshmi,' commented VK as we waited for the cab to take us to Concord Museum, described by its official website as 'The gateway to Concord's remarkable revolutionary and literary history'. It housed the oldest and most treasured collection of Americana in the U.S. Not surprising, for the Battles of Lexington and Concord on 19 April 1775 signalled the start of the American Revolutionary War.

The revolutionary history was represented by muskets, horn, pistols and other symbols of warfare, but it was the pacifist Henry David Thoreau's possessions that drew VK like a magnet.

'There are Emerson's artefacts too,' I offered a democratic reminder as we went around, but Emerson had to be satisfied with a cursory nod of approval as VK went around reading all the texts on Thoreau and memorising the great man's quotes. After a close look at the reconstruction of Thoreau's house in the museum upstairs, we started on the trek to Walden Pond.

Thoreau had lived in self-isolation for two years and his second book, *Walden: Or, Life in the Woods*, is based on that experience. The book's success made him famous enough to merit a public monument when he died in 1844 and that was what we set out to see. We started on the trail, but it was really cold.

VK, eager for that first glimpse of Walden Pond, strode

ahead with Amar, while Arpitha and I dawdled after, sharing a broken umbrella. The combination of cold weather and rain is a sure-fire recipe for misery. Luckshmi called to say they had reached but had decided against walking the trail since it was too cold for the kids. They waited there for a bit before going back home. I was so cold I wished I could turn into a kid and go home too.

VK's regular and enthusiastic references to Walden Pond and Thoreau's cabin made me visualise a small, picturesque pond with a delightfully cosy wooden cabin tucked near the bank. But then, having already got the hang of the American attitude to size, I should have been prepared at least for the size of the pond. For it was no pond, as I know ponds, but a huge body of water.

An awestruck VK was at the edge, drinking in the sight—there was nature's plenty to drink—before he bent down and reverentially cupped the water in both hands. I blinked in disbelief, for he is so sensitive to cold, he wouldn't, in normal circumstances, have dared dip even the tips of his fingers into such freezing cold water. The powers of adoration!

The small stones that were scattered about the sand bank made my hands itch to play duck and drakes. I selected a suitable flattish pebble, but VK guessed my intention and was appalled. 'No, don't. One shouldn't play here. Let's walk to the monument.'

I dropped the stone into my bag and followed him with Arpitha, who had gathered a few stones too. At the end of the half-mile trek, we found a heap of stones of different sizes. Nearby stood some narrow granite posts spaced out and forming a rectangle.

'Where's the monument?' I looked around.

'There's the monument.' VK pointed to the haphazard pile of stones.

Really? What a strange memorial. My curiosity was roused. VK, thorough on Thoreau, explained that Mary Newbury Adams, an ardent admirer of the conservationist, visited Walden Pond in 1872, ten years after his death, to find nothing in the woods to mark the place where the historic cabin had stood.

Dismayed, she got the idea of placing a stone from the pond to indicate the spot that was pointed out to her. Her suggestion that everyone who loved Thoreau should add a stone was enthusiastically taken up and soon a cairn grew there. What a novel method to move stones. If only we could use it to clear rubble around our place.

When the foundation of the cabin was discovered in 1945, just a few feet off the stone cairn, the granite posts were put up to indicate the exact area. This was a unique way to mark the site of a unique man's pilgrimage, or, let's call it hermitage. The solemnity and aura of the surroundings rubbed off on me. I placed the stone I had with me among the others. Arpitha offered one to VK. To our amazement, he refused to accept it, choosing instead to pick one up from the pile and pocketing it. 'A souvenir,' he mumbled, looking a trifle shame-faced, but, recovering quickly, he added an explanation to legitimise his unusual act. 'I'd read that people don't just add stones to the pile. Some take a stone or two as keepsakes.' Aha! A neat give and take policy that had prevented the molehill from growing into a mountain.

A large wooden board with Thoreau's quote stating the

purpose behind his self-isolation stood nearby. His words were heartening: 'I went to the woods because I wished to live deliberately, to front only the essential facts of life and see if I could not learn what it had to teach and not, when I came to die, discover that I had not lived.'

Bit by bit I understood why VK had a special fascination for the man who practised social distancing long before the pandemic, who preferred to put not six or eight feet, but a mile and a half between himself and other humans, the man who loved nature and was admired by Gandhi and E.O. Wilson whom VK admired too. The latter's work, *The Future of Life*, starts with a moving letter to Thoreau.

But soon it got biting cold and philosophic contemplation gave way to a very physical desire for warmth. We walked briskly back to Concord Museum to find Anil waiting for us and rushed into the warm car like cats seeking sunlight. Oh, for a beaker full of warm tea, I fantasised. And there, indeed, they were, cups of welcome, warm tea—a Boston tea party of sorts—waiting for us, thoughtfully provided by Luckshmi.

# Whale Watch

FOR ONE WHO HAD SEEN a whale only in books or on screen, and for whom Moby Dick was the last word in leviathans, I was as keen on the New England Aquarium Whale Watch as VK. Luckshmi's delicious idli-sambhar-chutney breakfast put us in the right frame of mind for a day with whales and dolphins. We could hardly wait to set out; yet, true to the pattern we had set for ourselves, we realised we would only be on time for the 12 o'clock trip.

Fortunately, it wasn't raining when we left, though thunder showers were predicted for the evening. We needed two vehicles and a cab was booked to play second fiddle to Anil's car. I found myself in the Uber with VK, Arpitha and Malavika, who couldn't be separated from her book of jokes. VK wasn't given a chance to prise out the driver's biography, for all through the ride she kept us entertained with a relentless volley of 'Knock, knock, who's there?' riddles. Only the cabbie tried to guess the possible responses, though Malavika wasn't really looking for answers. The cabbie began to look a little harried and I bet he'd have loved to fling this riddle at her, if he had been able to get a word in edgeways: 'Knock! Knock!' 'Who's there?' 'Voodoo.'

'Voodoo who?' 'Voodoo you think you are, asking all these questions?'

When we reached the harbour, we found there were other diversions in sight. I was captivated by a street musician performing on a saxophone and halted. A little boy was shaking a vigorous leg to the music, but other than the two of us, and the boy's parents who were fondly filming the scene to send it all over the world, no one around showed the slightest interest. Probably this was normal. Some people did contribute money, though, slipping a note or coins into a box kept for the purpose.

On the other side, a Black man was playing the trumpet and, very close to him, a White guy was doing the same. This was interesting. With my knowledge of the trumpet limited to the certainty that it wasn't a guitar or a piano, I tried to figure out whose music sounded better to my untrained ears. But I need not have bothered, for the two began judging each other. A quarrel broke out. 'Your music is all shit,' said the White musician. 'What about yours, man? Buggering crap,' the Black one retaliated. The argument sounded promising and I would have enriched my vocabulary too, but it was time for the whale watch, and I tore myself away with some reluctance. What was uplifting about the verbal duel was that both musicians stuck to their trade, exchanging insults only about the music; there was absolutely no other form of abuse—neither racial nor personal.

People were already queuing up beside the twin-hulled catamaran, 'Cetacea'. Perfect name for a whale watch expedition, cetacea being an order of marine mammals like whales and dolphins. VK and I followed A&A who had already booked the tickets online. Once inside, we prowled around, decided that the prow would best provide the wow view, and planted ourselves there. We noticed that the corresponding bow was already occupied by an excited group of children and two harried grown-ups.

The high-speed catamaran blazed out of the harbour, and with a stiff breeze accompanying us, we were on our way. We could hear the pleasant-voiced tour guide over the intercom welcome everyone and give details of the weather and the 3-to-4-hour expedition. We would go about 40 to 50 miles into the ocean before sighting the magnificent mammals, she said, adding that we'd be given free tickets for another trip if we didn't see any.

'Anticipatory bail,' I commented in a low voice to VK, and then shouted for he couldn't hear me; the wind had carried my voice away.

'What?' VK shouted back. 'Anticipating whales? Sure, but not yet. Be patient.'

'Not whale. Bail,' I wailed, then gave up and concentrated on the sea. Standing at the prow with Arpitha beside me, I couldn't believe we were rushing along the Atlantic Ocean. What a fabulous experience it was. The catamaran surged forward cutting through the ocean that cleaved, curled and bubbled under its assault. I could have stood there forever, with the wind on my face, the ocean stretching all around endlessly. At first a lurch, caused by an oncoming wave hitting the boat, took me unawares and I stumbled, but I quickly adapted to the waves and learnt to balance myself against the sudden roiling, reeling and tottering movements.

Arpitha began to feel queasy and sought refuge in the cabin. Amar spent the rest of the trip holding her hand and soothing her, while she rested her head on a table, much to the admiration of Malavika who was keeping her seasick mother company.

'Look! A whale,' the excited voice of the guide alerted us, and there was a ripple of excitement as everyone in the open portions of the catamaran rushed to the sides to get a good view. And the whales didn't disappoint us. They came in a pod and, as if they had planned to dazzle us with an impressive show, they showed off. They leaped, twisted, dived, somersaulted, sometimes in tandem, as we watched, bewitched. The guide gave distinguishing details about the whales and addressed them by their names. We should have been impressed, but we weren't really paying attention; all eyes were peeled to watch, photograph or videograph the spectacle. We had a whale of a time and were spoilt further by dolphins joining in. After we had had our fill of the marine creatures, the guide announced that we were turning back.

Now I began to feel a little dizzy. The waters had turned a little choppy—perhaps a sign of the predicted thunder showers coming on—and every time the boat roiled, my stomach churned. I thought food might make me feel better and so I went down to the cabin to get a couple of rolls of chappati and potato that Luckshmi had thoughtfully brought along. I felt worse in the closed cabin, and after a quick pat on Arpitha's head and a soothing word with Amar, I ate the chappatis and joined VK on the deck. The rush of fresh sea air on my face made me feel better immediately.

VK soon went to get his rolls and returned looking serious. He said the scene in the cabin wasn't very encouraging—people puking, sitting with heads bowed or looking green in the face. Arpitha and Luckshmi still had their heads down on the table. When the trip ended, they tottered out, already beginning to feel better. Looking back, I am amazed I didn't suffer as they unfortunately did. I am a sitting duck for motion sickness. I can only conclude that the novelty of the experience and the adrenaline rush it generated had kept me going.

The New England Aquarium was just a hop away on the Boston waterfront and who did we see waiting at the entrance but a lookalike of a dear friend, Mujib, who I believed, was in Canada. Then why was this man smiling so familiarly at us? Spending all that time in the sun watching whales must have addled my brains. Before I could shake my head to clear it, the lookalike was shaking VK's hand.

It was Mujib all right, not his doppelganger, and his friend, Madhav, was with him. The explanation of their presence was simple. Madhav was leaving for Seattle soon, and Mujib wanted to look him up before he relocated, but knowing we were coming to Boston, had planned his visit to coincide with ours. He wanted to surprise us and succeeded. He shocked me, in fact. He had been coordinating with Amar, whom he had taken into confidence, and had arranged with him to meet at the aquarium. Whoops of joy and introductions followed and soon we went inside after a quick hello to the Atlantic harbour seals that were on outdoor display and could be viewed for free. The seals looked like they were sulking. Understandable, after all who would take kindly to being an unpaid source of entertainment?

Unlike many parts of the U.S., the aquarium was teeming with people, and since there was every chance of getting separated, we divided ourselves into two uneven groups. Malavika was determined to be with A&A—their devotion to each other in seasickness and health had won her over completely. The rest of us formed the other group.

The gigantic, four-storey Ocean Tank at the centre of the aquarium would have taken my breath away if a kid hadn't already done that by butting me as I came in the way of his escape from his pursuing friend. I gasped, held my stomach, sighted the magnificent tower of water with its equally majestic occupants and gasped again. We hadn't even got over the sight of those playful whales and dolphins and here were these exotic sea creatures one had only heard of, all under one roof. There were different varieties of fish of varied colouring and size, penguins, green turtles, eels, barracuda, sea dragons, sea jellies ... The singular exception was the octopus whose fellow we had seen in a different form in Chicago. VK took one look, shuddered and turned away.

We were lucky it was feeding time. We witnessed the absorbing sight of trainers in wetsuits dive into the water to feed a variety of fish to the nun-like penguins waiting patiently on the cluster of rocks. We were told they were African and Rockhopper penguins who appeared to be in no mood to hop.

Who can miss Myrtle the huge green sea turtle, a healthy nonagenarian and the queen of the Ocean Tank since 1970, swimming about with majestic nonchalance, as if she was the last word in longevity and meant to hold the title forever. The fascinating coral reef at the top section of the tank, well, fascinated, while the Amazon rainforest exhibit gave us an enticing second-hand taste of the Amazon experience. We gave the Ray Touch Tank, where we could actually touch the rays or sharks, a wide berth, choosing instead to watch the electrifying sight of the fearless or the reckless try their hand at it.

By the time we came out of the aquarium, the two kids were fagged out. Anil and Luckshmi decided to take them home while the rest of us took a subway and walked around the Boston Commons. It began raining once again. After dinner at a restaurant named 'Prescient', we bid goodbye to the two Ms and took two trains back to Alewife where Anil was waiting for us. We reached home by 10, exhausted, and promptly tumbled into bed.

Amar had to get back to work and left for Neenah early next morning while we got ready for tours of MIT and Harvard. Luckshmi and Anil had taken the day off to take us there.

# MIT and Harvard

WE ASSEMBLED NEAR MIT FOR our walking tour. I knew it was a guided tour, but I wasn't prepared for a backwards walking guide. 'Hi, I'm Austen.' A guy with a ponytail introduced himself and waving to us to follow him, crossed the road walking backwards. I was tempted to try it, but discretion prevailed over foolhardiness.

Hearts in our mouths, we followed Austen, afraid he might knock into something or someone. But no, it appeared he had eyes behind his head too, for he never once broke his backward stride to check anything, all the while telling us about MIT.

He showed us around the classrooms and lecture halls, now walking forward, and lead us into the largest of them all, that looked like a mini theatre. I asked VK if I could sit on a chair. Before he could say, 'Don't', Austen, who had overheard me, said, 'Sure, you can.' And I did, gingerly, jumping up almost at once, as if I had committed a sacrilegious act. There was a huge blackboard too, and chalk powder near it. It seemed like an anachronism but the sight was heartening—it wasn't all technology at MIT.

Austen was well-informed and spoke clearly and

knowledgably. At one point, early on, he told us that courses at MIT were known by numbers. All regulars knew which school conducted which course. He gave some examples and then mentioned that there was no course number thirteen.

When he paused for questions at the end of that speech, VK asked, 'If MIT does not have a course with the number 13, what hope is there for human rationality?'

The question took Austen aback and he said nothing, maybe because a very tall, White senior citizen, turned to VK and said, in the tone one uses to a not particularly bright child, 'You see, 13 is an unlucky number.' Austen quickly moved on. 'Not much hope for human rationality,' I whispered to VK.

We tipped him discreetly and headed for Harvard, after a quick bite of the chapatti and potato rolls in the car. The Harvard guide was Laura, a plump girl in a micro miniskirt. She was good too but not as confident of the facts as Austen had been. I quite liked her as she took us around, though I'm convinced the men must have found her skirt distracting. VK wasn't so sure. 'Stocky legs,' was his comment.

'Uncle, careful. Body shaming not allowed,' Arpitha whispered.

'It was a compliment,' he grinned.

Harvard wasn't as well-manicured as MIT. The trees, the old-world charm of its red buildings, the general attractiveness of letting the grounds be, brought University College, Thiruvananthapuram, to my mind. Or, maybe I was plain nostalgic for my city. Laura took us around Harvard Yard, the oldest part of the picturesque campus, pointing out various buildings, the halls, the Memorial Church, the offices, the classrooms and departments.

She had introduced herself as a psychology student. So, when she pointed out the psychology department, VK asked her if she had taken any courses by the famous Steven Pinker. No, she answered, while pointing to a distant window where Pinker had his office. Strangely, she was more enthusiastic about Daniel Gilbert, Pinker's colleague in the same department.

She took us to the statue of John Harvard, considered the founder of the university, though the monopoly of the title has been disputed. In fact, the statue had an interesting anecdote behind it. Since no one knew how the seventeenth century clergyman had looked, a student had served as the model for the sculptor, Chester French, who was also inspired by other portraits to produce the final effect of a wistful John Harvard on a chair, an open book on his lap and a few more under the chair. I thought he looked pensive, probably wondering why students and visitors kept rubbing his left shoe to keep it polished and gleaming. 'Why not my right?' he seemed to ask, sticking it out.

Ah, we could have told him why. And had the superstition extended to include the other foot, he'd have been sporting a pair of well-polished shoes. Of course, Arpitha and I faithfully adhered to the Neils Bohr principle again with a quick rub of the right toe. I gave a surreptitious pat to the dull left, which was feeling left out, before catching up with VK who had stomped ahead in some disgust. We found many of our tour companions openly tip Laura. Her skirt had won many admirers, but, alas for Austen's ponytail. We added our bit and bid her a happy goodbye.

'Where next?' I asked Luckshmi.

'Lexington Common,' she replied promptly. 'You can't come to this city and not visit it.' If the host thinks so, then so be it.

Once we got there, we understood why Luckshmi had insisted on a visit to the place. Lexington Common or Lexington Battle Green was where, on 19 April 1775, the first shots that triggered the American War of Independence were fired. Strolling around the spacious, sedate and attractively green public park, it was difficult to imagine that any war could have begun there. Apparently, Concord also found that difficult to believe, certain the shot fired at the Old North Bridge in Concord that afternoon was 'the shot heard round the world', as R.W. Emerson had put it, and was the actual origin of the revolutionary war. With both Lexington and Concord battling for the honour of hosting the inaugural battle, and celebrating 19 April as Lexington Day and Concord Day respectively, the date was diplomatically declared Patriots' Day. I was secretly pleased to learn that such momentous debates, on which all of history hinges, took place in the U.S. too.

The bounds of this national historic landmark park were dotted with several plaques, memorials and statues, notably those of Captain John Parker who led the small Lexington force in the skirmish, and the Minuteman. The Minuteman statue symbolically represented all the Minutemen who confronted the British forces, Minutemen being the name given to local colonists who were willing to take up arms at a minute's notice. We also gazed with curiosity at the oldest war memorial—a granite obelisk, the Revolutionary Monument—that stood as a tribute to the first casualties of the war. I was glad they called the obelisk an obelisk and not a needle.

After a quick look in at Cary Library, the local library in Lexington, which, like the other libraries in the U.S. left me drooling, we returned home. Amar called with the wonderful news that he had got an offer from Bed, Bath and Beyond. What lay beyond was a whole lot of formalities to go through before the job became his.

Though Amar wasn't with us, we celebrated with dinner at Holi Restaurant, run by a couple of impatient Indians. But the food was good and on returning, we finished our packing in a tick; the perk of living out of suitcases. We were all set for the next leg of our trip that would take us from the east coast of Boston across several states to California in the west. We were going to spend a week in San Jose.

We had to take the early morning flight to San Jose via Chicago. The alarm, chosen the previous evening for its unignorable ringtone that mimicked the final gasps of a man being strangled, made me shoot out of bed at 3.30 next morning, hair on end, to find Luckshmi already up and making coffee for us, the sweetheart.

Our goodbye to Luckshmi and Anil turned out to be a long goodbye as the Uber cab, scheduled to reach at 4.30, didn't come on time. We spotted the car on Arpitha's app about half an hour away from Luckshmi's home. It was moving in mysterious ways its wonders to perform. With twenty minutes to go, it stopped abruptly. After that, it just refused to budge. We grew frantic. 'Is there any way the app can make it start? Try,' I appealed to Arpitha urgently.

We began thinking of last-minute options when

it appeared to move again. Soon it arrived, with a loud squealing of brakes. A merry woman at the wheel jumped out to help us with our bags. 'Sorry,' she grinned. 'I had to take a-call-of-nature break. Will make up, don't worry. Early flight? No problem; can take you there in a jiffy with my eyes closed.'

'Eyes closed?' I was alarmed. What followed easily awarded her the top spot as our most interesting Uber driver in the U.S. She needed no encouragement to open up and talked as fast as she drove. She had a regular job as part of some government social security scheme that involved calling on aged citizens who were living alone. She needed a break and had taken a few days off to drive an Uber. She drove all night and would be back home when it was time to wake her kid and prepare her for school. Her husband was asleep and did not even know she was out driving.

'Is it safe? Driving all night?' I asked. She knew how to look after herself, she said. 'Once,' she continued, with a hiccup, 'I threw out a bunch of giggly, drunken girls at night and in the middle of nowhere. Yeah, their behaviour was unacceptable, hic.' Uber had accepted her explanation.

Keeping her promise, she drove with her eyes closed while we held on for dear life. Going dangerously close to a swanky SUV, she overtook it, explaining, 'I have my techniques for getting through heavy traffic. Hic. Look for a rich person's car, a fancy, gleaming affair, spot a little gap and flash past them. Rich guys are worried about their paintwork, and let you pass.' She giggled.

She giggled so much, VK commented later that the stop before she picked us up was probably not to dispel stuff from her body but to ingest some. Whatever it was, she got us to the airport on time all right. We pulled body and soul together, thanked her and raced to the lengthy queue at the security, dragging our bags behind. An official came around, checking tickets and directed us to another, much shorter, queue. Had they pulled out suspicious looking passengers and clubbed them together, I wondered, getting the heebie-jeebies once again. But it turned out to be the other way about—Arpitha found out that the special queue was to facilitate security for low-risk passengers. Aha, one look at us and they had decided we had water on our brains.

Security went like a song, though Arpitha's bottle of water created a minor hiccup. The three-and-a-half-hour flight to Chicago was on time and when we reached, I had to set my watch back by an hour. And once we reached San Jose, I had to set it back by a further two. Uff! The exasperating time zones of America. I am all for the one country, one time zone policy.

Those people who argue for multiple time zones in India too ought to be sent to every nook and corner of the U.S. They will be cured of this desire forever.

The gate to board the next flight to San Jose was pretty close and we were divided into groups for boarding. We were in group five, the last group. VK quipped that we were the low risk and low priority passengers. 'Group five, you may please stay back. We are loaded to capacity.' This flight was on time. California, here we come.

# San Jose

THE TRIED AND TESTED METHOD of following a couple of other passengers on landing at San Jose let us down. The carefully selected group we trailed led us to the wrong exit, and their good work done, dissolved into the day before we could appeal for guidance. After a mini bumbling peregrination, a helpful man directed us to take a shuttle to the right one where we had to collect our baggage. And who should we find waiting there but Nizar himself. The looks of delight were mutual.

With broad grins we went to the luggage belt to find only my suitcase and Arpitha's enjoying the rattling roundabout ride on the belt. Oops. The last of the Mohicans, we concluded; everyone else must have taken theirs and reached home while we had lost our way. We quickly yanked them off the belt like superheroes just in case we were fined for coming late—one never can tell with America, but, what do you know? It turned out ours were the first pieces of luggage to be offloaded.

The belt soon brought along bags of six and more dimensions but we had to wait ages before VK's suitcase showed up like a coy bride. We soon joined Nizar and were on our way home. The weather was cool, the company was great. Nizar couldn't believe we had actually made it halfway across the globe. He blinked, incredulous, and looked at Arpitha in admiration. We told him to keep his eye on the traffic.

Nizar's wife Shaheeda had prepared a delicious lunch for us before leaving for office and we fell upon it like, er ... starving Delta passengers. We had been served next to nothing even on the long flight from Chicago to San Jose. The second flight had a couple of airhostesses marching up and down like the Gestapo and flinging miniscule packets of biscuits or peanuts at those of us monkeys who weren't asleep. It was a quick 'blink-and-you-miss-it' delivery. Two unfortunate teenagers three rows ahead who had chosen that moment to flutter their eyelashes at a good-looking guy across the aisle and missed catching the gimlet eye were left gazing wistfully at the handsome peanut-munching hunk.

The evening was for walking. Shaheeda, a wispy, pretty pocket edition and a lovely person, returned and, just as we had done at Rajive's, we went on a bracing walk around the neighbourhood. I can't help mentioning yet again how pleasurable walks in the U.S. are—clean air, picturesque scenes, no garbage and hardly any people to bump into. With no walls to block your view of neighbours' gardens, we gaped and gasped at the flowers in full bloom, especially the roses that appeared to be high on the popularity list.

Nizar has the Western attitude to time and no one can beat him in punctuality. When on his annual visit to Trivandrum, he would call to say he'd come over at 5, you could be sure he would be at the doorstep at 4.59 so he could place his hand on the doorbell at 5. It's another matter that there would be Third World problems waiting to foil his plans—the power would have failed, the doorbell wouldn't ring, but he'd have no idea, and finally the power of his lungs would help him get our attention, 10 minutes after 5.

Be ready at 9, he had told us, very gently, when we had finally retired for the night. And we were ready at 10.30, an hour and a half being our normal handicap. He understood this soon enough and indulgently made his adjustments. Shopping first, he said.

Nizar wanted us to get to know his beloved country as best as we could in a short time, so he had planned visits to giant shopping malls. He took us first to an unbelievably huge store, 'Costco Wholesale, San José', where he had a membership of sorts. Everything in Costco cost a lot. And we could buy only in giant quantities. Nizar acted like a good guide as we explored the indoor giant spaces. You don't need to buy anything, he consoled us, just look at the place, just look at the choices one has. So we looked.

We went to another enormous mall next, stuffed with stuff and people slowly pushing their laden shopping carts. I cannot even begin to describe the sheer scale and variety of things available. We walked and walked along miles of aisles, so broad people could keep to the right even as they shopped and not bump into others as they dropped.

We were spoilt for choice; that's the problem when there is the world's plenty before you. Or should I say China's plenty? But we did buy gifts for relatives and friends, taking smart advice from Nizar on what to get.

The sprawling parking lots complemented the gigantic malls—so huge and well concreted that planes flying overhead would be tempted to try their wheels there, and get some shopping done too.

It was here that one of the mysteries we had mulled over at the beginning of our trip was solved—where were all the people? Well, here they were, calmly pushing shopping trolleys, queuing at cash counters with the patience they showed while driving on storm-hit roads and leaving with mountains of shopping in giant cars often described as 'trucks'. This was one big, self-satisfied nation. And profligate too.

'Maybe malls are where the heart of the nation lies,' I observed to VK later. 'Not in Walden Pond.' Sorry, Thoreau; apologies, E.O. Wilson. 'It's in these massive, incredibly well-organised, cornucopian covered spaces.'

VK nodded, looking rather sorrowful, and added, 'Just as India's heart does not lie in Sabarmati ashram or a pair of British designed spectacles.' Continuing in the same vein, he said, 'Remember, this is the real reason why the Soviet Union collapsed. They may have launched the Sputnik and built nuclear reactors, but the only things they could mass produce were propaganda and misery. Just rumours of these malls must have done more to undermine the system than all the James Bond-type things the Americans may have done.'

On the way to the Rose Garden, Nizar spoke about something else that was an eye-opener. People bought so much they did not have room in their homes for all of it. Therefore, they actually hired storage, in places built for it, so they could keep those things that were spilling out of their already well stocked homes. A second home just for stuff! Nizar did not say this but he seemed to imply that the market could be relied on to find a solution to every human problem.

The Rose Garden proudly proclaimed itself 'The Finest Rose Garden in America', what else? I decided to believe it, for it was fabulous. There were roses all over the place, of all colours, sizes and smells, or no smell at all. This was before Covid came along, of course, to make you head to the nearest PCR testing centre if you couldn't smell a rose.

After a quick dash home for lunch, Nizar took us to Stanford University—the place that had produced one U.S. president and any number of Nobel laureates, and the new Twitter chief Parag Agrawal too. It was close to Silicon Valley, about 20 miles from San Jose. It is such a special feeling, to step into these hallowed universities that one has only read and heard about.

Stanford has one of the largest campuses in the U.S. A few students were cycling about while we walked around the huge quadrangle, and strolled into the quiet Stanford Memorial Cathedral that stood at the centre of the Quad. Coming out, Nizar pointed out the lecture halls. We peeped into one, and visited the book shop on the campus. Nizar led us out and to the car.

'Guess where we are going next?' Nizar asked, as we piled in. He should have known better than to pose this question to someone who is geographically challenged. Seeing my confusion, he offered a hint. 'A place very close.' He had seen VK studying the local map the previous day, so he might have thought the clue would work. Alas, I'm not a map person, so I remained baffled. 'You'll see your favourite there ...' he tried again.

'Got it,' I beamed and came up with a convoluted guess. 'The beach. The fish. Fish curry is my favourite.'

Nizar gave up. 'The closest beach is almost 30 miles away. We're off to Google's headquarters at Mountain View, just 5 miles away, and ...'

'Google.' I goggled. 'Really? Oh, and Shaheeda works there. My favourite person.' I felt like an idiot.

'Googleplex is the name Google has given its sprawling campus,' explained Nizar in the car. 'A combo of Google and complex, and also a play on the word "googolplex", "googol" being ten ...'

'Raised to the power of a hundred,' I chipped in, keen to redeem myself.

'Exactly,' Nizar said with a nod. 'To indicate its hugeness.'

'Like all things in the U.S.,' VK butted in.

Shaheeda was waiting for us. 'I'll get you your visitor's pass,' she said, and led us briskly to a computer in the centre of the hall. There we caught The Efficient Mr Google napping. Glitches succeeded glitches. Info fed in would either not be accepted or disappear when she moved to page two on a touch screen device. Finally, after many heroic attempts, when everything was done and the print pass instruction given, the machine refused to oblige.

'To have this happen in Google,' I giggled.

'Our Indian Railways has better operating computers,' VK teased.

'Let's try another computer,' Arpitha offered a techie's suggestion.

'Yes, let's.' Shaheeda gave Arpitha a grateful glance and we went to a sorry-looking computer abandoned in a corner that perked up on seeing us. 'Use me,' it begged.

We did, and it worked, if not like a charm, at least like a wannabe witch's first shaky spell. With the pass adorning my neck, I was all set to go inside and nose out the search engine's secrets, when I found Shaheeda shepherding us out of the building. Maybe the more interesting section is in another building, I thought, since it had more than twenty buildings. But no, we were going to the cafeteria that I soon discovered was the most interesting section for everyone working there.

'You must go to the cafeteria,' the security chap advised.

'Aren't you taking them to the café?' a colleague of Shaheeda's asked after we were introduced.

'What shall we have today?' I overheard someone ask, when a group of three passed us.

'We're going to one of the most famous cafés here,' Shaheeda announced and as we walked there, she described the different cuisines on offer.

On the way, we saw two or three young men juggle clubs. 'To keep the staff healthy,' Shaheeda said. 'Google cares about its employees. We have swimming pools, gyms, game tables, video games facilities. Or they can cycle, juggle, you name it.'

'Is this recreation time for them?' I asked.

'No, it's work time. But they have the freedom to go for the occasional break when they feel like it. So that it feels like home.'

'What fun,' I thought. How diverting if the principal

of my college had brought in such a reform. 'Teachers, henceforth when you feel drained, you may indulge in some juggling. I will give you time in between classes for that,' she would say. And when she announced, 'Teachers! It's juggling time', we'd all prance out of the staff room with balls, clubs or rings. The more daring ones might bring blunt knives along. And we'd juggle in the corridors or out on the grounds. Would there have been more students to watch me juggle or to listen to my lecture? Would they have decided my true talent lay elsewhere, say, with the circus?

My ridiculous reverie ended, for we had reached the cafeteria. We had to wait in a long queue to get the much talked about food, and when we finally got it, I wanted to tell Shaheeda her cooking was better any day, but didn't—I didn't wish to dampen her enthusiasm for the café.

The campus had a college air about it, maybe because it had a lot of young employees, just out of college, and probably very pleased with all the perks Google offered. After walking around for a while, we left for Susan Cheryan's house.

Susan Cheryan was the girl with the curl, not only in the middle of her forehead but all over her head. I first met her when she was in class IX and I was her English teacher, fresh from college. She was an endearing, intelligent girl and a vivacious prankster. I still remember the heavily scented love letter she and her equally mischievous friends, Philo and Sudha, had sent me after I left the school. It was neatly typed on an attractive letter paper. I had taught them letter-writing and they had followed all the rules. 'Timbuktu' was the name of the place while the date was 'Half past kissing time, time to kiss again'. Signed 'From an ardent admirer', it arrived in an equally fetching envelope. I had accosted VK, a little coyly, with it, and he had replied, sounding a little put out, 'Why should I send unsigned letters when I'm sending signed ones? And the stink!' He sneezed twice, closed his nose and closed the matter. I found out who the perpetrators were only years later when one of the trio confessed.

Susan and I had stayed in sporadic touch and when she got to know I was in the U.S. and was actually coming to San Jose, she wouldn't hear of my not visiting her. She sent me her address and we decided to meet.

Nizar offered to take us there. Arpitha and I went in Shaheeda's car while VK went in Nizar's. Shaheeda drove fast and competently, but her conversation with her niece on the phone while driving kept me on the edge of my seat till we arrived at our destination.

Without any sort of coordination both cars slammed the brakes at Susan's at the same time. She rushed down to welcome us. I was seeing her after a long time, though the years sat lightly on her. We were overjoyed to meet each other and some time went in squeals, shrieks, hugs and pecks—social distancing was an unknown phenomenon then. The others stood around looking uncertain, until we remembered them and effected hasty introductions. The house and its sprawling surroundings offered ample proof that nature lovers lived there. It was set on a hill top and built on different levels. Flowers and trees abounded and if you climbed the steps to the top you'd get a fabulous panoramic view of the surroundings.

Susan's house is huge, and so is her dog, misnamed Pebbles. He is a very singular dog and should have been christened 'Boulder'. He was excited to see people—doesn't see too many of that breed, apparently—and showed it by jumping on us. As always is the case with dogs, he too, with unerring instinct, selected me as his special target. Nizar kept a polite distance and told us later that he had a dog allergy. I told him I had it too, and while his made him sneeze and sniff, mine made me leap on tables and chairs.

We met Susan's husband, Suresh, a quiet person who speaks through his hobbies—growing bonsai, keeping bees, making tables and doing other carpentry. Her older daughter was there too, a very pretty girl. Susan is a terrific cook and her culinary skills were on display at the fantastic spread she had got ready. We returned to Nizar's with a feeling of deep joy and contentment.

Nizar had planned the itinerary with great care. It was good for us that he was working from home; and this was pre-Covid—talk of foresight. He was an engineer who had given up his job at Microsoft to set up his own company. Being his own boss, he could give us all his time. He was the perfect host and the perfect guide. He had actually bought filter coffee powder and unearthed the decoction contraption, under the notion that we love filter coffee. I do like filter coffee, but only when someone else makes it for me; otherwise, I'm very contented with Nescafe Classic instant coffee. That had been our great indulgence when our salaries were paltry and we really had to plan our expenditure. Nescafe cost a king's ransom, but we willingly gave in to the blackmail.

He told us the previous evening that our next destination was Yosemite. Now, if you haven't heard about the place, you wouldn't have the foggiest what the other person was talking about. And I hadn't. I know, I know, I have been hopelessly ignorant, as ignorant as an American is of India.

Yousmiti? Yoursmi ...? for often people swallow the last syllable. I felt reluctant to ask and expose my lack of awareness. Anyway, I would find out the next day, spelling, pronunciation, geography and all. I knew it was a national park, though.

It's an overnight stay, Nizar clarified, and it'd be cold. We quickly packed in extra warm clothes. He said he was lucky to have got us a room in a hotel, and I wondered what the big deal was. We never had a problem anywhere. Later I realised that it's a favoured spot for tourists and Americans, and one had to book months in advance. He managed to book a tent in the outdoors for himself. It was a brave decision on his part—a wonderful host putting his guests' comfort above all else—for he could easily have had a wild bear for company in the night.

We left for Yosemite at 9.30. Yes, we actually set out at 9.30—Nizar's devotion to punctuality finally shamed us into being on time. It took us about five hours, lengthened because of the mandatory breaks—a bathroom break, a petrol break and one for lunch. The journey took us through different terrains—barren mountains, fruit orchards, and acres and acres of land with no people about.

VK, seated beside Nizar, was in conversation with him all the way, often crossing swords about politics. It was all friendly and often funny, but the two sides never came together or even gave signs of budging. Nizar was a free-market enthusiast. He had endless complaints about the bureaucracy, not just in India but also in California. Do you know how horrible the power situation is in California? Big government is to blame. Any idea how long it takes to get permits to repair your roof? Nizar would frequently pepper his arguments with quotes from Ronald Reagan and jokes about the old Soviet Union. VK would counter with stories of private sector corruption and inefficiency.

'How can this sort of landscape lead to a national park?' I asked, when the two paused to breathe, and, as if on cue, we entered the wooded area. A river showed up—the Merced River—and became our companion, bubbling along on the side, and the heat of the plains gave way to a cool, bracing temperature. Huge trees wished to hold us in close embrace, and gigantic granite rocks loomed over us. Waterfalls greeted us and when we reached Yosemite, in Mariposa County, we were totally bowled over.

We checked into Yosemite Lodge. A comfortable wooden room had been allotted for us on the first floor, with a big cosy bed and a neat bathroom. I immediately initiated a mini disaster. I went to inspect the washroom and the tap I turned on wouldn't close. I appealed to the engineers and Nizar managed to stop the flow of water, but what I had begun, the other engineer, Arpitha, completed for, after she used the bathroom, the tap refused to obey anyone's entreaties or force. Water gushed out.

Nizar called the desk while I stood guiltily about, certain that this time we were going to be sued. What damages would they clamp on us? Would we be allowed to return to

India or would we have to languish unwept, unhonoured and unsung in the U.S.?

The desk responded promptly by sending a plumber who examined the tap from all angles, getting quite wet in the process, and pronounced it was the tap's fault. Hurray! It was an old one and would be fixed soon. The Americans are honest people, I thought, relieved. We left him to it and went off to explore the place and, though American honesty had just been on display, we weren't taking chances, and took with us all our essential papers, money, cards and wallets.

We took tour buses to a couple of scenic spots before returning to the hotel to set out on a trek. I took a long and admiring look at Bridalveil Fall visible from the hotel front and wondered at the bride the veil hid. After completing the trail, we were debating on what next, when a tall, elderly man stopped—stooped would be more accurate—in front of our group. He smiled and asked, 'Indians or Pakistanis?'

'Indians,' responded VK. 'Look at these engineering geeks,' he pointed towards Nizar and Arpitha.

That opening exchange led to an interesting conversation. The gentleman had once taught mathematics at Chicago University but quit, after twenty years, and joined the State Department, where he worked for the rest of his career. He let us in on a little secret. He was stationed in New Delhi in the Eighties, organising raids in Afghanistan. 'What? We were neutral in the war. Besides, we were chummy with the Soviet Union,' VK said.

'That's what everyone thinks,' he countered. Apparently, there was cloak-and-dagger stuff that involved India and the

U.S. and our professor friend was right in the thick of it. He had been stationed in Pakistan too. Ooof. I rubbed my hands. Actually, I was feeling cold, but he gave me a pleased smile.

VK later remarked that very few people in the States can distinguish between Indians and Pakistanis. He repeated the joke about the old couple in North Carolina who met a neighbour, a young Indian, at a party. 'You are not from around here, are you?' asked the man. 'No,' said the Indian, 'I am from India.' 'How nice,' the lady exclaimed, 'Is that outside North Carolina?'

Our professor friend asked a lot of questions and reacted very warmly to Nizar when he explained his start-up. Nizar designed and fabricated something called 'embedded systems'—state of the art, custom-designed ones that the Chinese could not duplicate. His clients included CERN, NASA, ISRO and the European Space Agency.

Nizar was also as American as the U.S. flag. Shaheeda had told us he once had a sticker on the back of his car that read 'I was not born here, but I got here as quickly as I could.' In Seattle, where he had accepted U.S. citizenship, his voice resonated over all the others when he took his oath with a thundering, 'I do!' startling everyone else into stammering their oaths. Such was his patriotism he refused to use Chinese components in his devices, even though it would have been cheaper and profitable to do so.

The professor chuckled when he heard all this. He obviously approved. It was wonderful to meet us, he said. He lived a retired life in California and spent much of his time visiting national parks. Rarely got a chance to meet Asians, he added.

He asked VK to recommend a good book on ancient Indian history. VK beamed and suggested one by a U.S.-based scholar—*Elephants and Kings* by Thomas R. Trautmann.

When the professor mentioned Chicago again, VK asked him if he knew Saul Bellow. The professor said in a dismissive tone, 'Yeah, used to see him around the place.' Clearly not a favourite.

'Why,' asked Nizar, 'given your love of mathematics, did you ever leave Chicago?'

'It was too cold,' said the professor.

Nizar spotted a chance to score a goal. 'Took you twenty years to find that out?' The professor joined in the laughter, laughing loudest.

As we shook hands and said our goodbyes, we noticed a tiny lady seated on a bench nearby, like Patience on a monument. 'That's my wife,' he said. She had sought a seat as soon as we began our conversation and had not uttered a word at any point. I empathised.

After parting ways, our group trekked to the waterfalls—a splendid sight, but then we had seen Niagara. We attempted to get the spray on our faces; not a good idea for we got a little soaked and it was already getting very cold, though the temperatures didn't get as low as the phones had warned. Even snow had been predicted. When we returned, we found the errant tap fixed.

After dinner, we went to bed by 9.30. Nizar left for his tent. This was the first time he would be spending the night in a tent and he didn't know what or whom to expect. We wished him luck—that it would only be tame animals that came to socialise with him.

The next morning, we were relieved to see Nizar at the restaurant, whole and dapper. He didn't have a harrowing tale to narrate, of wrestling with bears, shooing off bobcats and being kept awake by howling coyotes. 'Pleasant place, the tent, and very comfortable.' His eyes twinkled.

'No close shaves?' I asked.

'Oh, yes, had one,' he quipped, stroking his chin. 'And a refreshing bath too.'

It was now bitterly cold and we were grateful for our sweaters, thick coats, mufflers and monkey caps. Wishing to avoid the multiple-choice questions I'd face if I asked for a sandwich for breakfast, I went for pancakes, and so did Arpitha. They were not a patch on the ones in Chicago—my touchstone for excellence. VK and Nizar had eggs and toast.

We returned to our room for it was time to check out. We'd just exited with our bags when I rushed back in. VK was certain I had left behind my wallet; Arpitha thought it was my sweater. I joined them soon, shoving a pen into my bag. 'Has Yosemite stamped on it,' I said to their baffled faces.

'You'll end up like the free souvenir-seeking chap in *If It's Tuesday, This Must Be Belgium*'. VK rolled his eyes. 'And then I'll pretend I don't know you.'

'What happens to him?' Arpitha, who hadn't heard of this late Sixties movie, was curious. She wasn't, by a long shot, going to the pictures or anywhere in the picture at that time.

'His suitcase bursts open and the souvenirs tumble out.' I laughed. 'How do my two miserable pens compare with that guy's collection? He had taken the telephone from the wall and even a lifebuoy from a boat.'

VK snorted while Arpitha chuckled. We checked out, and drove to view the falls from different angles, or, rather, in an attempt to find the road that would lead us to the Tunnel View, we ended up going round and round in circles, staring at the waterfalls from every side, and each view was as wow as the next. Sometimes it was the same wow ... er ... view. This was an occasion when I was actually grateful we'd lost our way. We finally stumbled upon the right route. I don't know what I expected when I heard the name Tunnel View—analogy made me imagine a narrow view—but a splendid spectacle greeted us when we drove out of the Wawona Tunnel. Waw!

Nizar was a trifle apprehensive of the swirling mist that accompanied us, believing it could mature into a fog and then what would we see? Maybe then it would have been a tunnel view in the actual sense, but we were lucky, for the mist that played hide and seek heightened the allure of the breathtaking scene. Once the car was parked, we rushed to ogle at the sprawling valley with the two granite wonders— Half Dome, a rock formation that looks like a dome cut in half on the left, and El Capitan or El Cap, a 3,000 feet vertical rock formation, a challenging temptation to rock climbers, in the centre with Bridalveil Fall, our old friend, to the right looking more coy and captivating in the misty garb.

'This, to me, sums up Yosemite,' I took a deep, blissful breath and said. By now I was very familiar with the name, rolling it off my tongue with great ease, while swallowing the final syllable with a silent, fashionable gulp.

On the return journey, Arpitha and I slept quite a

bit while VK and Nizar continued their amicable verbal sparring. We had passed a lot of fruit farms on our way to Yosemite, and I had told myself we would look them up on our return journey. The stalls attached to some farms looked so appealing we got Nizar to stop at one, brushing aside his tip-off that fruit was cheaper in his neighbourhood. The multi-coloured luscious fruits were very tempting. There were apples, cherries, plums ... all looking juicy and inviting. A very made-up girl with red cheeks and lips that put the apples and cherries to shame was at the counter. Strangely, VK didn't notice the heavy make-up, or even the girl—he had eyes only for the cherries.

We bought a couple of kilos of cherries and plums and before Nizar could even restart the car, had our hands in the bags. He politely declined our offer, and we were thrilled—a cherry refused is a cherry gained. We polished them off before we reached home, much to Nizar's amazement. He watched, fascinated, when I turned the bags upside down on the off chance there could be an errant cherry hiding in the crinkles, but we had done our job of gobbling them up only too well. 'Greedy pigs,' he must have thought, though what he said was, 'You must really love them.'

✱

That evening we met a few friends. Nisha Pillai and her husband were the first to visit us. VK and I had got to know Nisha while conducting quizzes and eventually became friends with her. She was an excellent quizzer who used to represent her college—The College of Engineering,

Thiruvananthapuram, familiarly known as CET—and won our respect for holding her own in a male-dominated sphere. She had now settled in San Jose and we were delighted to meet her and her husband who worked for Google.

We had hardly bid them goodbye when Yasmin, the daughter of a very close friend, Sheila, dropped in with her husband and their two young sons. The two boys promptly dropped off to sleep over each other on the sofa and had to be carried off when they left. It was so good to see Yasmin— we had practically watched her grow up into a beautiful young woman—and her family. She brought us melt-in-the-mouth cakes she had baked that we finished off even before her car had turned the corner.

If it was Yasmin that evening, it was Yasmina who pandered to our palates the next day, earmarked for visiting relatives. 'Visiting relatives can be boring' is a sentence I'd often used in class as an example of lexical ambiguity. But it turned out to be unambiguously enjoyable when we visited two of my nephews and their families who lived on opposite shores of San Francisco Bay. They were meeting Arpitha for the first time, which made the visits extra special.

Nizar, ever obliging, dropped us at the apartment of my nephew Afzal in Sunnyvale where Yasmina, Afzal's wife, served a mouth-watering spread that was calculated to make us gain weight even before we left their place. When not munching, VK spent much of his time trying hard to get their sweet, frisky little daughter, Inara, to stand still for a photo. He didn't succeed; we have only blurred images of her as memories of the visit.

Laden with gifts and bursting with good food, we

staggered into an Uber that Afzal had arranged to take us to Fremont where Haris, another nephew, lived with his wife, Shabana, and their three children. It was years since we had met them. There's a special joy when you meet loved members of the family so far away from home. It was tea time when we arrived and VK predicted we'd be served tea that ought to take care of dinner, and he was spot on. We returned to Nizar's, satiated in every sense of the word, and crashed straight into bed.

*ƒ*

Susan had suggested we drive to Carmel-by-the-Sea and we did just that the next day. It was a Sunday which meant Shaheeda, the workaholic Google-ee, could come along too. In case you haven't got it, Carmel-by-the-Sea is a city called Carmel that is by the sea. Intelligible to every American and to me. Imagine the confusion if they had named it Carmel-by-Pelagos or Carmel-by-Mar Pacifico.

We had seen the Atlantic; now the Pacific beckoned. I don't know if we stared at it like stout Cortez and his men did, not having had the privilege of seeing them stare, or seeing them at all. Besides, Keats had got it all wrong. But I was struck silent all right, for I tripped and slipped to the sand from a rock. I stifled my involuntary cry; I didn't want the others who had gone ahead to know. VK was already cupping the sea water in his pacific hands, almost as reverentially as he had the water from the Walden Pond.

Carmel-by-the-Sea is a city beloved of artists, which explains the picturesque houses we saw along the way. Doris

Day of 'Que Serà, Serà ...' fame, lived there post-Hollywood. People still remember that Clint Eastwood had been the city's mayor for two years, though they may not know Japan's capital, such is the sway of the tinsel world.

It is a dog-friendly place where hotels welcome guests with dogs or dogs with humans at the end of a leash. High-heeled footwear is banned there—too many people tripping on uneven pavements and way too many lawsuits in consequence, which probably is the real reason, not the twisted ankles. I had just proved that one didn't need high heels or an uneven pavement to take a tumble, but whom could I sue? That rock? The Pacific Ocean?

Coming back to Carmel, believe it or not, to this day, it has no street addresses. Most houses have legendary names like 'Hansel' or 'Sea Urchin'. Desiring to retain the quaint 'villageness' of the place, the founders decided on doing away with street numbers, parking meters or street lights outside the downtown commercial area. So how does one find a house in Carmel, you ask? Go down the lane next to the big tree, take a turn where there's a rose bush, keep going till you reach a cottage with two dogs, big windows and blue curtains. The rose bush might have disappeared. They may have changed the curtains. A dog might be missing. But that's the one.

The nearby Monterey Bay Point Lobos State Reserve is famed for its sea animals and birds. 'See, a sea lion! A sea otter! And a seal!' I squealed, though I couldn't really make out the difference between a sea lion and a seal, pinnipeds, both. The seal I had spotted turned out to be a sea lion, lying immobile, as if sunbathing. We realised it was ill when a uniformed man approached us to ask if we had seen a lone sea lion on a rock. Yes, we nodded, thrilled to point it out. The man took a close look and then asked us to move back, not realising we'd have had to do a backward flip into the Pacific to obey him.

The animal was injured and it was a risk even allowing people near it. The uniformed chap turned out to be from the Marine Mammal Rescue Service. Despite feeling sorry for the seal, we were quite elated to witness an actual rescue. We had seen so many exciting rescues in documentaries, we couldn't wait to see the real thing. And wait we did, our patience tested for it appeared as if those involved were playing out the drama of rescue in slow motion. After watching the creature from a safe distance for what seemed like eternity, a girl from the rescue team took slow and studied steps to go close and observe it for a bit, before moving back, more slowly, if that were possible. When I watched the Derek Chauvin trial recently, the slow and deliberate way in which the lawyers inched to the main point reminded me of the sea lion rescue.

A silent bunch of tourists had gathered to watch the rescuers who were watching the stricken creature. No one fed it or petted it or helped it in any way. After some time, we got the impression this was a Buddhist monastery and not a part of the U.S., if the constant cry of sea birds and the lapping of the sea on the rocks could be imagined in a monastery. What was the intention of the rescuers? Slow death for the sea lion so that they could carry off the remains and report a daring rescue that failed? We decided to leave; we'd have had to wait forever to see the full rescue, if at all. And then someone would have to cart our stiff bodies away; rigor mortis would have set in.

We proceeded to other points on Point Lobos. There were plenty of vehicles. We had to queue up to get parking slots and traffic crawled near the beach and the parks. The drive along the Pacific coast was great; not an inch of the landscape was anything less than beautiful. But it was different from Door County. As we drove past a great number of golf courses, I wondered if the famous orange-faced man had played at any of them.

If you drive along rural Kerala, the scenery would be equally breathtaking. Only, the billboards and the houses abutting the roads, in a melange of colours, shapes and sizes, would hide most of it. If you wanted relief from the hideousness of some of the buildings and turned your eyes to the roadside, you'd see mounds of litter and plastic. Roads, it was said, made possible a ribbon development. In India, it was a ribbon distribution of plastic and other waste.

How come the Americans kept their country so clean? Nizar waxed eloquent on cleanliness and order being natural attributes of the world's best country and people. VK observed that what was well done was the collection of all the rubbish generated—and an incredibly huge amount was generated—all of which was exported to Asia. One did notice that there were rubbish bins everywhere.

In places like Wisconsin, there was no sorting of waste. Everything was destined for landfills. The waste generated at Amar's flat—from food waste to discarded footwear or packaging—had to be dumped in a huge plastic bag, sealed and left on a rack in a shed. Every two days a huge truck turned up at his apartment complex. The driver did not even get off his seat. The shed was opened by remote control, the bags scooped up by a giant arm and deposited in the innards of the truck, doors banged and that was it. The truck did not have the smell characteristic of garbage trucks in Kerala, which signalled their presence to a wide circle around wherever they moved. People pinched their noses shut while birds and strays danced about joyously when these trucks turned up.

New York and California had some kind of sorting at source, but it was not an easy system to follow. If you bought a cup of coffee, it was served in a paper cup, as tall as a bucket. But you could not throw it into the bin marked paper after use. It had to go into the one marked 'other' because it had a plastic lining which prevented it from being processed with used paper. There are more 'other's in this world than philosophers or post-modernists dreamed of.

There were problems with waste disposal but New York and California were at least thinking about it and trying to improve with some sort of recycling policy. But India, we realised, was now following the U.S. model. Single use plastics had swept aside the old waste-not-want-not culture. Much of the garbage festooning our roadside and pavements was such plastic. We consumed plastics like Americans did, only we could not dispose of it like the Americans. For we were in Asia; where would we dump it? We were the dump.

'Look at oil,' said Nizar, switching topics. 'A short while ago we imported much of it. Thanks to the vigour and creativity of our private sector'—he was speaking of fracking and new oil fields—'we are now a net exporter of fossil fuel. There is a bonus,' he added, 'the Saudis and Russians cannot arm-twist us.'

'Short-sighted thinking,' countered VK. 'You are ruining the Earth and instead of leading the world in fighting global warming and mass extinction, you are letting greed and short-term political goals dictate policy.'

Nizar and he still agree to disagree on these matters, often over international phone calls. These conversations are often friendly arguments and though they are conducted with much good spirit, neither VK nor Nizar is willing to give in an inch.

We got caught in a huge traffic jam—our first experience of one in the U.S.—but it was a very disciplined one. Nizar took a route home that took us along some more picturesque houses and beautiful scenes, and we dropped in at Madhav's house on the way.

# San Francisco

THE NEXT DAY WAS RESERVED for San Francisco. We left by 10:30—you guessed it, the scheduled time was 9—and took a heap of warm clothes along since Nizar's smart phone predicted a temperature of 13 degrees there. Past experience had built in us a healthy respect for U.S. weather forecasts. But Murphy's Law butted in and this time the temperature soothsayer messed it up.

'It's going to be cool,' Nizar had announced as we started off but it turned out to be warm the whole day and we couldn't resist keeping Nizar warm round his ears by rubbing it in. In fact, this was the first day in all of our trip I spent outside without a sweater. It took us about twenty minutes along the rather picturesque Interstate 1-280 to reach Moffett Federal Airfield, more familiarly known as Moffett Field.

'What is that?' I gasped, catching sight of what appeared to be a gigantic bird cage in the middle of a huge airfield. 'What monster bird does it house?'

'Did it house, you mean,' Nizar looked pleased at my open-mouthed astonishment. 'The bird has flown. This is Hangar One, one of the world's largest free-standing structures. It housed an exceptionally unique monster bird, the USS Macon.'

'USS Macon?' I racked my brains. Hesitantly, I asked, 'An aircraft carrier?'

'Yes.' Nizar looked pleased. And I was relieved. The geographical faux pas of a couple of days ago still embarrassed me.

'An airship, actually,' Nizar clarified. 'Like Hindenburg. But with improvements.'

'Yet it crashed,' I couldn't help commenting. I had begun to recall some details. Nizar gave a wry smile and added more information. USS Macon, once called 'the Queen of the Skies', and its sister naval airship, USS Akron, were two enormous helium-filled aircraft carriers built by the U.S. Navy in the 1930s to carry Sparrowhawk fighter planes for scouting.

In October 1933, a few months after a thunderstorm aided the crash of Akron, Macon shifted its base from New Jersey to Moffett Federal Airfield, then known as NAS Sunnyvale. But it wasn't all sunny. In 1935, it met the same fate as Akron when a storm tore into it, forcing it to sink into the sea off the coast of Big Sur in California. It kept its resting place well-hidden until, in 1990, the wreckage was discovered underwater at Monterey Bay National Marine Sanctuary. But the exact location remains a well-kept secret. The twin disasters sounded the death knell for the U.S. plan for rigid airships.

'Macon must have been so HUGE,' I exclaimed.

'More than two and a half football fields in length,' Nizar read out from his phone. With Google having taken over the place, it was only fitting that we sought the assistance of its search engine for details.

Metal structures rarely have the captivating appeal of natural wonders, but the sheer size of this one inspired reverence and, as if by common consensus, we remained silent for a while, gazing at the bare skeleton-like structure that had once sheltered and showcased a magnificent man-made machine. I don't know what the others were thinking but my musings moved on to the vulnerability of the inventions of man, however incredible they might be, when pitted against the might of nature.

My thought air balloon was pricked when Arpitha, who had been looking very contemplative, as if troubled by a deeper philosophical concern, turned to Nizar and asked, 'Is there a restroom hereabouts?'

This was nature on a different call, and once it was heeded, we motored to the Golden Gate Bridge, another superb metal structure. That drive was quite an eye-opener for we couldn't help but notice how different the houses in San Francisco were from those in Wisconsin and other places we had been to. Where we noticed the luxury of space in the latter, San Francisco houses appeared to be drawing comfort from hugging each other. It brought to mind Malvina Reynolds's song, 'Little Boxes', popularised by the American singer and social activist, Pete Seeger—little boxes that 'all look the same'.

Arpitha and I gathered from the conversation between VK and Nizar that space crunch continues to be a huge problem in San Francisco and harks back to the time of the Gold Rush, when the limited land that was available struggled to accommodate a suddenly exploding population. Since it is surrounded on three sides by water and the fourth by San Mateo County, the city cannot expand; it can only reuse its available space, and identical houses packed close together has become the norm. This has resulted in some unenviable records—San Francisco has America's highest rents and the country's most expensive real estate. A totally lop-sided income equality balance has only augmented its problems.

But these disturbing facts were pushed aside when we sighted the Golden Gate Bridge, considered one of the wonders of the modern world by Americans and an engineering marvel by the rest of the world. This suspension bridge, the darling of photographers, that connects the city of San Francisco to Marin County, California, had been the subject of so many picture postcards sent long back by relatives in the U.S. in those good old snail mail days that I expected a long, gleaming, golden bridge. Instead, the 1.7-mile-long icon of San Francisco was clothed in undistinguished dull orange, fashionably elevated to be called 'international orange'. I learnt later that it had been the colour of the primer when the steel arrived but the consulting architect knew a good thing when he saw one. Realising the colour would be much more visible than the red and yellow that had been originally planned, he had decided to keep it.

'Then why call it golden?' Arpitha, equally disappointed, asked.

VK knew the answer to that one. 'Simple. That's because the strait it spans is called the Golden Gate Strait.'

Now that we had got that straight, we sat back to enjoy the drive over the bridge.

'Alcatraz! Alcatraz!' VK shouted, pointing into the distance, as if he had sighted an old friend.

'Who?' Arpitha looked puzzled. 'The guy in Tintin? But isn't that General Alcazar?'

'No, no, there. That island. Alcatraz, isn't it, Nizar?' VK asked. 'Where America keeps its best and brightest and never lets them escape?'

'Yeah,' Nizar laughed. 'But not any longer. That's the dreaded prison, Alcatraz. The Rock.'

'Welcome to The Rock,' I quoted from the Sean Connery movie, and again we became collectively speechless; this time it was an uneasy silence as we took in the grim island and the impregnable buildings sitting on it that had housed America's most notorious criminals.

'Now it's a museum,' Nizar broke the silence. 'A popular tourist destination.'

'Much better than a permanent destination,' VK commented.

Our next destination, though, was the Point Bonita Lighthouse, a mere twelve-minute drive from the north side of Golden Gate Bridge. Any lighthouse visit involves a lot of huffing and puffing, mostly as you climb the steps to the top. But Point Bonita that is on the continent's edge makes certain you don't take even the journey to the lighthouse lightly. You have to pay with your sighs, exclamations and the occasional expletive for there is a steep and rocky half-mile trail to negotiate, and a tunnel and a suspension bridge to cross before you reach the lighthouse. And the fact that it was crowded, it being Monday, one of the days when it was open to the public for a few hours, didn't make the trek any easier.

But so what? You are treated to breathtaking sights of the bustling, unpacific Pacific, frolicsome seals and cormorants on rocks, and stunningly colourful wild flowers along the way that might take your breath permanently away if you don't watch your step as you stumble along the edge of sheer drops.

I was thrilled to glimpse Alcatraz again. The Golden Gate Bridge, viewed in its entirety, had a special allure from that distance. The architect had a point choosing orange as the colour. On one side, the city of San Francisco beckoned. The working lighthouse, built in 1855, sitting solidly on its rugged foundation, was more special for its history than for its looks, but the spectacular panoramic view of the ocean from its vicinity compensated.

The climb down was invigoratingly strenuous, helping us work up a great appetite by the time we reached the car. But, alas, lunch turned into a very distant possibility for, in trying to steer clear of the heavy traffic that Nizar predicted would be on the road, we got caught in the mother of all traffic jams—one that could easily have given Bangalore's worst a run for its money.

Finally, Nizar managed the impossible and I expected him to sigh and announce, 'Phew! Now let's look for a suitable restaurant.' Instead, he said, 'Now let's give the Nike missile site a look in,' and vroomed us to SF-88 where we did look in, from the outside, for the site wasn't open to the public that day. But even that was enough to send a chill of fear down our spines as we recalled the Cold War years and the kind of deadly missiles the place would have housed as defence against possible Soviet bomber attacks.

Sufficiently sobered by these reflections that put paid to our appetites, we nonetheless stopped at a restaurant for a light late lunch before we settled down to enjoy the hour-long drive to Napa Valley, the home of vineyards. 'We're going to Domaine Carneros,' Nizar announced.

'Superb!' I responded. 'What's that?'

The story goes that Napa Valley was catapulted into heady heights on 24 May 1976 when two little-known Californian wines were adjudged tastier than the more famous French wines at a blind taste testing in Paris and the event, christened 'The Judgement of Paris', brought instant world fame to the vineyard capital of California. One small sip for wine tasters, one giant leap for tourism. Sadly, the recent fires in California have resulted in some of these wines having an added flavour of smoke. What the expert wine tasters would make of it is anyone's guess. Maybe award more prizes.

I was totally mistaken in my belief that wineries would resemble factory buildings with vineyards nearby. So, when we stopped at what looked like an impressive chateau, I thought this was a picturesque stopover before we went to Domaine whatever. Imagine my surprise when I was told that this WAS the domain of the winery.

'Why, kings and queens should be living here,' I exclaimed. 'Not barrels of wine.'

'Haha, in a sense, you are right,' Nizar conceded. 'Domaine Carneros is modelled on an eighteenth century French castle.'

Tours were closed that day, though we were told wine was available inside for tasting. But, alas, this information didn't exactly pep us up. We were a group of non-drinkers, who needed only water to get high. What brought a sparkle to our eyes, though, was the beauty of the place as we walked around; there was so much to see and gasp over—the beautiful, beautified gardens, neat walkways lined by coiffured hedges, unique fountains and the lush vineyards nearby. For connoisseurs of wine, Carneros vineyards produce the perfect Pinot Noir and Chardonnay grapes, the key grapes in champagne and sparkling wine. Well, so I'm told. Thankfully, Domain Carneros escaped damage during the horrific 2020 California fires, but I read that one of its vineyards was burnt down.

We took the Interstate 1-880 back home and reached at about 7.30 in the evening. Considering we had packed so much into one day—visits to an airfield, a bridge, a lighthouse, a Nuke site, a pseudo castle and vineyards—we weren't tired, and surprisingly, the man who drove us everywhere and pulled us into and out of traffic jams appeared as fresh as he had been when we started in the morning.

Susan and her husband came over that evening and joined us for dinner. Susan brought delicious banana cakes and that was the beginning of a beautiful friendship between the two families. Food was the catalyst. Nizar returned the container with some delicacy he had prepared along with a box filled with some pastry Shaheeda had baked. That box had to be returned, and, well, you can guess the rest.

'Hi, Arthipa!' Susan hailed Arpitha. She just can't get

her name right—she calls her Arthipa, Apritha, Athripa, Arithpa, Apirtha, anything but Arpitha.

'Why don't you shorten it to Arpi?' Nizar suggested. 'Then you can't go wrong.'

'Brilliant idea.' She jumped at it, and turning to Arpitha, said, 'I'll call you Apri in future.'

# Big Basin Redwoods State Park

SHAHEEDA, THE CONSCIENTIOUS WORKAHOLIC, left for Google to do justice to her pay cheque while Arpitha decided to stay back citing she had to catch up on some 'pending work' which, I strongly suspect, goes by the name 'Amar'. Therefore, it was VK, Nizar and I who left the next morning, if you can call 11 am that, for Big Basin Redwoods State Park.

'It's California's oldest state park. Established in 1902,' Nizar said as we clambered into the car for the hour-long drive. He fixed his coffee mug on the cup holder near his seat ritualistically before taking the steering. I really don't know why he carries a monster mug of coffee on every journey, for I've never seen him take more than a sip from it. Maybe the proximity of caffeine is enough to give him the kick he needs to drive long hours with ease and zest.

Our trip to High Cliff State Park in Wisconsin had given me a taste of America's state parks, or the state of parks in America, but nothing prepared me for the majesty of this mind-blowing 18,000-acre park. Though there were other trees like oak, pine and fir, it was redwood, named so because of its reddish-brown bark, which overwhelmed us. The mammoth trees, some more than 2,000 years old and over 300 feet tall, grow here because the combination of summer fog, moderate temperature and winter rainfall is perfect for them. If you want to know just how insignificant you are, spend some time at Big Basin.

Once Nizar parked the car opposite the Visitor Center, we set off on the short trail, home to some of the tallest and widest old growth redwoods, our spontaneous noises of appreciation startling the bird population around. We walked into the quiet and sedate forest, sometimes together, sometimes in single file, but never straying outside the trail. We often stopped to examine and gush over some tree or place that demanded special attention, like a sawn-off section of an ancient redwood that had tags to indicate growth rings from the tree's birth in 544 AD to modern landmark dates. What excited us was the reference to India. The tag said, '544—tree sprouted in California. Chess played in India.' Here was a tree just planted in California, and in India people were pitting their wits against each other at chess. Excellent.

There were giant trees named 'Mother of the Forest' and 'Father of the Forest', though labelled offspring weren't anywhere in sight. Feminists will rejoice to know that the mother, at 293 feet, was taller than the father, a mere 251-footer. Trees with huge hollows invited us to step in and I learnt later that the hollows were caused by fires. Early settlers found them a convenient place to house their geese and other domestic animals, thereby giving the hollows the name, 'goose-pens'.

While on the subject of fires, we were shocked and

saddened when we heard about the horrific destruction in Big Basin caused by the CZU Lightning August Complex fire in 2020. Big Basin was not a stranger to fires—the low-intensity fires actually kept the forest healthy—and redwood trees with their thick, flame-resistant bark are equipped to withstand them, but this one was a conflagration apart.

It burnt down the Visitor's Center and other historic buildings, extending over all the 18,000 acres of the park. Environmental experts believe that this fire followed the same path of the most destructive fire before this—the 1904 blaze—creeping along the same ridges and pathways as it moved through the park and the mountains. But though the redwood trees burned their hearts out, most of them have survived and green stems have been spotted protruding from the tree trunks, proving the veracity of the second part of their scientific name, 'sequoia sempervirens', meaning 'ever living'. The cleaning and re-building process is on and experts believe the resilient forest will in time regain its past glory, with a marked increase in the number of goose-pen trees.

Not being clairvoyant, we were clueless about the devastation awaiting the forest whose refreshing sights and sounds we were soaking in. We came across a clearing among the trees that looked like a sylvan amphitheatre with unsophisticated but solid wooden benches around. Who knows, it might have been the scene of a stirring dramatic performance of King Lear or Julius Caesar in the past.

It was a great trek, and we enjoyed the walk so much we didn't realise how much distance we had covered. We switched from a small trek to a longer uphill one, and other than meeting a couple intent on not reaching the bottom earlier than expected, we met no other human. It was only us and nature. There were any number of small wooden bridges to cross, some with dead trees doubling as bridges, though there wasn't much water in some of the brooks. Rather disappointing, that.

Nizar had a fascinating metal walking stick with him—fascinating because it had a compass on top. 'Great walking stick,' I said, examining the compass with curiosity.

'Not a walking stick, please,' he implored. 'Makes me feel old. This is a hiking pole.' He said he generally found it hard to keep his balance and stay upright during descents, so a walking stick, sorry, a hiking pole, is a good prop and prevents a fall.

'It's best to descend sideways,' VK offered expert advice that he immediately demonstrated. 'Helps you keep your balance.'

'Ha, that'd only help me fall sideways,' Nizar quipped.

When we returned to the starting point and checked the board, we found we had actually done a moderate trek and that, combined with the first shorter one, meant we had walked a total of 9 miles—not bad at all. We took a look at the famous Auto tree with a hollow into which people had driven their cars in the past, before we prepared to leave.

We were getting into the car when a woman approached Nizar and asked for a lift for her husband, Chris. 'Sure,' said Nizar.

Chris soon appeared and flashed a half smile at all of us before climbing into the front seat. He had an interesting story to relate. He was one of the 'Boat People' we had heard so much about. He had left Vietnam as a boy of fourteen, spent two weeks on a boat, was rescued and then spent six months in an Australian refugee camp. He was then taken to California and resettled.

America had welcomed him and he embraced America with a passion. He became a computer engineer and was working with Cisco in San Jose. Though he had married a South Asian woman, the family was, like Nizar, uber-American. One of his kids was in college, but had taken the year off to explore the country with her partner. They were all out on a trek and had left one of their cars at a park over 20 kms away and walked to Big Basin. Crazy, very American family, we thought. Imagine spending your holidays trekking and sleeping in the open, when you could have stayed at home and read or watched movies. And probably got on each other's nerves. They intended to trek back but he needed to get something from his car.

VK asked him about the journey out of Vietnam. 'I hardly remember,' he shrugged. 'And, frankly, I don't want to'. He had never tried to trace any of his relatives in Vietnam. 'Nothing to be gained by revisiting the past,' he commented.

Well! In a world focused on identity and roots and all sorts of complicated, often narcissistic, attempts to discover one and uncover the other, here was a truly free bird. Chris had embraced the work ethic of his adopted land as well as its mores on relaxing and recreation. He thanked Nizar profusely when he realised that Nizar had discreetly changed his planned route to drop him very close to where his car was parked.

That evening was our last in San Jose and we played cards and dined with a tinge of sadness. We were going to miss Nizar and Shaheeda who had made us feel so much at home. Nizar's generosity and thoughtfulness continued till the last for he came to our room with a monster suitcase to take to Neenah.

'But this is too huge,' I protested.

'Try stuffing all your shopping into the suitcases you had brought,' he gave a knowing grin.

I didn't even try; I was appalled when I began pulling out from the cupboards a never-ending collection of fat, shapeless carry bags. The giant suitcase got filled in no time.

'Here's a gift for you,' Nizar handed something to VK.

'Wow, a walking stick,' VK enthused. Nizar grimaced.

'A hiking pole,' I quickly corrected VK who reiterated, 'A walking stick, of course. What hiking, viking pole?' I'm glad he's not in the diplomatic service.

# Back in Wisconsin

SHAHEEDA SERVED A DELICIOUS BREAKFAST and I gave
a satisfied burp as I bid the lovely provider of great food a
solemn goodbye. Nizar drove us to the airport, accompanying
us in, and left only after he saw us safely in the line for
security. What a warm, caring, perfect host. Wistfully, I
watched him move away.

My attention was drawn back to matters at hand when
a security guy shouted, 'Over seventy? Come to this line.' I
thought he was looking at me and was quite miffed. Over
seventy and me? Why I was barely ... A Chinese woman
who was behind me immediately moved to that line, and I
gawked. She didn't look a day over thirty. Lucky Chinese.
They never seem to age.

We were taking the United flight this time, to
Minneapolis and from there to Appleton, and it turned
out to be much better than Delta, which isn't saying much.
When I went to collect my hand baggage after security, I
found my handbag sitting in solitary splendour on a side
rack. My heart sank. What now? I thought I had been
very cautious with its contents, but turns out I wasn't. The
culprit was fished out—a packet of samosas Shaheeda had
given us.

'Ah, food!' the guy said, in a tone that implied, 'Indians!' He gestured to me to claim my bag.

The flight was on time. And we actually got something to eat—a packet of almonds, a cup of coffee and water too, which all added up to a lavish spread, by domestic flight standards. There were three airhostesses, all looking over seventy, definitely not Chinese, and very nice, especially the one whose attention we drew to an overhead luggage cabin that wasn't closed properly. She smuggled us an extra packet of almonds.

At Minneapolis we put the clock forward by two hours and during the flight to Appleton, when nothing was served since the flight was short, I drank in the sight of the sturdy Black airhostess chewing gum non-stop and occasionally blowing bubbles as a diversion. It came home to me that I might not see a similar sight for a long, long time. This was our last domestic flight in the U.S., and our trip was coming to a close.

༄

The final week was a leisurely one. We kept things easy with only two actual outings. The rest of the time was spent watching movies or crime serials, going on long walks in the evening and eating out at times. It rained occasionally, once again reminding us that bar a few dry days, the rain had been our faithful companion all the way.

In the three weeks we had been away, Neenah seemed to have re-invented itself. When we had left, the weather was cold and the trees had looked shamelessly bare, denuded of leaves. But Neenah welcomed us back with gentle warmth, lush hedges, trim, green lawns and trees richly canopied with healthy leaves. This made our evening walks very enjoyable, and with days being very long, our walks became long too. We'd return home at 9 p.m. when it was still bright.

We hardly saw anyone else walking, but people in cars would nod, smile, and if we wanted to cross the road, would stop for us to do so. Walking was so stress-free—unlike at home where even if you were on the pavement, it wasn't a walk as much as a challenging steeple chase, what with slabs missing, occasional mounds of garbage, heaps of sand or gravel, dry twigs, confrontations with two-wheelers or cycles, cats that dash across, dogs that play dead, not to mention dog poo that doesn't have loving owners to clean it.

One of our two outings was an afternoon visit to the EAA (Experimental Aircraft Association) Aviation Museum, one of Amar's favourite haunts. He hadn't missed any air show there when he was in Neenah. Amar and VK's passion for aeroplanes is amazing. I remember VK taking Amar to the airport when he—Amar, not VK—was a little child, as if they were going on a picnic, with water, chocolates and some snacks, to spend the whole day there. The new stringent rules at airports don't allow that any longer, but by then these two had spent any number of blissful days there.

Arpitha booked an Uber for VK and me; they would join us in the evening. The Uber arrived and wouldn't you know it; it was Gary again. Gary, we learned on our last ride with him, had spent all his working years as a 'water engineer' in California. Unlike Wisconsin and the states near the great lakes, California had a problem with water and so had to conserve the little it received and use what it had carefully. Gary ran filtering plants, largely for agriculture, different from those for potable water, he pointed out.

Perhaps Gary would help VK solve the problem of dead fish around Neenah. For one last time, VK asked about the dead fish in Lake Winnebago.

'Well,' said Gary, after mulling over it a bit, 'I am not sure I know the correct explanation, but I have a theory. Lake Winnebago is an artificial lake, a reclaimed swamp.' True. I remembered the exhibits in the natural history museum at Milwaukee about that and the life of the indigenous people around it before the White man redesigned the marshes and the swamp. 'So, no part of Lake Winnebago was deep; probably the deepest part was around 15 feet. This year was exceptionally cold and the cold extended to early spring. Winnebago froze over and stayed frozen longer than usual. My guess,' said Gary cautiously, 'is that this year the layer of ice extended deeper than usual. That would have decreased the amount of oxygen in the water. The fish probably died because they did not get enough oxygen.' He added that one had to get this confirmed from a scientist who knew more about fish and their life cycles.

VK listened almost open-mouthed. He had asked so many people; most of them had brushed off the question with a shrug or a brusque, 'Don't know.' Now here was a suggestion that seemed not just plausible, but correct.

When we got off at the EAA Aviation Museum at Oshkosh, a twenty-minute drive from Amar's apartment, we wished Gary and his mother well and thanked him for all the rides and his friendship. He smiled the way conservatives in America do, in a manner that combined warmth and distance. Not like Sue's smile. But he was a really nice man.

I had been so focussed on waving Gary goodbye that I left my black sweater on the car seat. I discovered the loss only when I felt cold inside the museum. I called Arpitha to tell her. I thought it would be a mere formality getting it back, but I learnt later that it entailed a long, protracted process. You have to pay 15 dollars to recover anything left behind in any cab, after establishing your bonafides. Daylight robbery.

I bet I could have got a decent new one for much less, but I would still have loved to get back my old sweater; it had been my most faithful companion all the way. Besides, I still had all those dollars in my wallet. However, the lengthy process and the trouble I'd put Amar and Arpitha through made me gulp and give it up for lost. I consoled myself with the thought that when Gary found it, he'd be happy I had heeded his advice to always take a sweater along, though of course he never advised me to leave it behind in cars.

A doddering old man, who appeared as ancient as the Wright Flyer, volunteered to show us around but my not yet doddering companion, whose eyes had lit up at the sight of all those planes around, hastily declined the offer. 'No, thank you, we'll make our way about.'

'Sure,' the man smiled, happy to vanish from our lives.

Whatever VK might have paid for the tickets, the museum experience was worth much more. You have to hand it to the Americans, to have created this phenomenal storehouse of aviation history with such meticulous care. If

I, whose knowledge of planes begins and ends with their ability to fly, could find it so absorbing, it was no surprise that an aviation enthusiast like VK was beside himself with child-like excitement. The replicas, the actual planes and scale models all got their deserved share of attention.

'There.' VK pointed. 'An F-100 Cockpit Trainer.' And I learnt it was a plane, not a person.

'Look.' He dashed to a Fokker triplane replica.

I dashed after him and read the history of the triplanes, regarded as the dashing 'knights of the air' during WWI. 'How romantic,' I trilled.

'Not when they were shot down,' VK said matter-of-factly, throwing cold water on that fanciful thought. He rushed to a Blériot XI monoplane and gushed, 'Louis Blériot flew across the English Channel in 1909 in a Blériot monoplane! And do you know what the press said?'

I could read, so I said, '"England is no longer an island."' He laughed and we moved to the next plane.

We saw the fabulous collection of historic airplanes, with replicas of the Wright Flyer, Charles Lindbergh's 'Spirit of St. Louis', the WWII planes, the war artefacts, pictures of war heroes and their stories stoking special interest. We saw in passing, the KidVenture gallery and had just stepped into the store for some mementos when the store attendant asked us to hurry; the museum would close at 5.

VK and I were surprised. Almost 5? We hadn't realised how time had flown. When we left the museum, I began to feel the cold once again. A&A arrived to pick us up and Amar, the Bostonian turned Wisconsinite, gallantly gave me his jacket. We wound up the day with dinner at Olive Garden restaurant.

# Shakespeare in Chicago

THERE WERE ONLY TWO DAYS to go for our departure when A&A came into our room, grinning from ear to ear. 'Tomorrow we're going to see Macbeth,' Amar said.

'Who? A friend?' I asked. 'Never heard you mention him before. The names parents foist on their children! Must have been teased a lot in school.'

Arpitha hooted. 'The play *Macbeth*, Aunty.'

'At a proper Shakespearean theatre in Chicago,' Amar added.

VK and I looked at A&A, open-mouthed. An actual play at an actual theatre? What a thoughtful, delightful surprise; the perfect icing on the cake of our U.S. trip.

Amar had booked tickets at Chicago's famous Shakespeare Theater. *Macbeth*, Shakespeare's bleak tragedy, was the one on offer that season at The Yard, one of the venues of the Shakespeare Theater at the Navy Pier in Chicago. What was more, one of the directors was Teller, of the famous comic-magician duo, Penn and Teller.

We left at 10 the next morning and Amar drove expertly to cover the almost 300-kilometre distance to Chicago in two and a half hours. Google maps helped us reach The

Chicago Shakespearean Theater without any problem, the tickets helped us gain entry and we stepped into the premises as if we were entering a sacred grove. But immediately after, our bodily compulsions kicked in; Arpitha and I were hungry and also wanted to use the washroom. 'Sacrilege.' The horrified expression on VK's face spoke volumes. 'Is food all you can think of, when we are getting ready for intellectual nourishment?' But Shakespeare, I'm certain, would have approved of our pandering to our basic instincts.

VK and Amar remained at the theatre; not wishing to miss the lecture by the directors before the play. When Arpitha and I entered the theatre again after our successful foraging expedition, they were waiting at the entrance, looking a little sheepish, for the lecture was at another venue. We were too satiated with good food to crow over them and at 1.30, we were allowed entry into the actual venue, the Courtyard Theater.

The brochure got it pat when it advertised the show as 'an eve of magic and mayhem', for that was precisely what we got. The theatre looked—there is special emphasis on the word 'looked' here, because everything could look like something else in a jiffy at the Yard—like an enlarged version of something like the Globe in Shakespeare's London. All wood, octagonal seating arrangements, thrust stage, upper stage and galleries all around. The additions to Shakespeare's theatre were the winding staircase to the left, small lights, a curtain at the back, and the fact that it was an indoor theatre and fully air-conditioned.

We were in the front row of the gallery—excellent seats that gave us a perfect view of the stage as well as allowed us to look down, literally, I mean, on the audience seated below. It was a full house and the show began sharp at 2 p.m. with a short welcome by Teller telling everyone to switch off their mobiles and let the place become eerily dark. 'Now you won't be able to call for help,' he laughed.

We were super impressed with the performance. With the exception of a few improvisations, and forays into casual modern language like, 'Thanks!' by Macbeth when he hears that he's been made Thane of Cawdor, Macduff and his family being played by Black actors, and the comic porter scene being very contemporary with the porter entering from the back of the theatre and hobnobbing with the audience as he walked up the aisle to the stage, the producers and directors had stuck to the original plot and Shakespeare's stylised language.

The performance was slick, the change between scenes so smooth at times it was like watching a movie. There was magic in the air all right. We willingly suspended disbelief and watched in wonder as Teller, a master of illusion, made the three witches and their cauldron disappear as if a blast of wind had blown away some smoke. We gasped when the dagger appeared floating in the air, shuddered when blood stains suddenly showed up on tunics, only to vanish with the same ease, and Banquo's ghost startled us by appearing on the chair with a sudden 'pop'.

We applauded with great enthusiasm when the actors lined up after the performance and realised only later that the rest of the audience had given them a standing ovation. I hoped nobody noticed this breach of etiquette. Our senses satisfied, we left the theatre to confront reality once again and began looking for restaurants and restrooms.

We spent the rest of the beautiful evening at the famous Navy Pier that had a major role to play in WWI and was now a popular tourist attraction. There was a stiff breeze and a lot of people were strolling about, but the Pier never gave the impression of being crowded; it absorbed all the people as if Teller had a telling role to play in it. We took a ride on the giant Ferris wheel, a key attraction, and though it gave us a superb aerial view of the surroundings, it was so sturdily built to safety standards that it was boring. The thrill one experiences on a Ferris wheel ride in India just wasn't there.

In India the experience is out of the world and rarely leaves you unscathed. It's always best to write your will before venturing on a ride. A rather rickety, squeaking contraption groans and takes you up slowly. The descent that is a signal for high-strung fellow riders to begin screaming in fear coincides with a hollow feeling in the pit of your stomach. Encouraged, the wheel cranks up its speed in unholy glee and gives you three hair-raising rounds before you alight, piecing body and soul together. Sometimes, when it is in a particularly sadistic mood, it stops just when your carriage has reached the top and is tilting for the descent, leaving you precariously perched there, not trusting the metal safety rod to protect you if you spill out. Just when your hair begins to turn grey and your whole life passes before you, the wheel starts moving and you return to safety.

We stepped into a Children's Museum—no, children were not being exhibited there—and also took a quick walk around the Crystal Gardens. We watched kids play at a lovely fountain and stepped into a couple of souvenir shops where I managed to pay with my stash of cash when the attention of the others was elsewhere. We walked along the length of the Pier, peering at the occasional statue there, and reached the other end where the anchor of the famous USS Chicago, a WWII navy vessel, was displayed. The breeze was stiff but not as cold and sharp as the blast that had hit us when we landed at Chicago airport. In fact, it was cool and bracing; so just walking about was a treat in itself.

'We're going to Devon Street next,' said Amar, chuckling as he drove us there. 'It's called "Little India" in Chicago.' The moment we entered it, we knew why. There was a Gandhi Electronic Store, showrooms with mannequins wearing ostentatious, glittering salwar suits, dosa outlets, an overflowing drain, bits of paper scattered about and some garbage on the road side. Nostalgia trip. And a sort of prelude to our return. An authentic Indian dinner at Woodlands rounded off the Indian experience and we turned back, savouring the long drive along lonely stretches under clear skies.

# Goodbye and Thank You

THE LEISURELY FINAL DAY WAS spent packing, weighing the suitcases, unpacking, repacking and weighing them again. The process was repeated multiple times before we were satisfied the weight of every bag was within permissible limits.

Amar was working from home but earlier, the night before, I had noticed him once again huddled in a corner with a book. It looked suspiciously like the one he had been swotting up before his job interview.

'Another interview?' I asked, perplexed. 'A job beyond Beyond?'

'Yes,' he nodded. 'A back up. In case the Bed, Bath and Beyond job doesn't work out. Getting a work visa is always a problem.' And if he got another offer, I for one wouldn't mind. I then wouldn't have a problem telling people where he works. Surely there can't be another company with such a suggestive name.

It was 5 June 2018 in the U.S. When we reached India it would be 7 June—we would lose the day we gained when we went to the U.S. All evened out. We left for O'Hare International Airport at 3 p.m., and Amar reached us there by 5.30, the time we had planned to reach, in spite of the exceptionally heavy traffic. A&A came in with us and once the bags were weighed and okayed, I felt at ease for I didn't really trust the weighing scale at Amar's—it never could make up its mind about the weight of the bags, or me for that matter.

We got our boarding passes and moved to the queue for security check, while A&A waited nearby. I kept glancing at them with love and gratitude; they had gone out of their way—Arpitha even accompanying us to California—to make our U.S. experience truly memorable. Then the long queue stopped moving. It seemed there was some serious problem, for a sniffer dog was brought in. Of course, the moment it sighted me, it jumped for a quick sniff at my ankles, drawing everyone's suspicious eyes to me, before it was made to remember by a tug on its leash what it was there for, and dragged away. The problem must have got solved for the line began to move and the dog gave me a little yelp of recognition as it bounced past us.

A&A and others who had accompanied passengers were now asked to leave, and looking rather bright-eyed, we waved them goodbye, watching till they disappeared from sight. Security went without a hitch and we boarded the flight.

Through the window we could see the sky wrapped in the hues of a spectacular sunset. America was giving us a colourful goodbye. We watched and watched till the plane took off. We were going home....